CW00703941

infoRock

The History of Rock Music

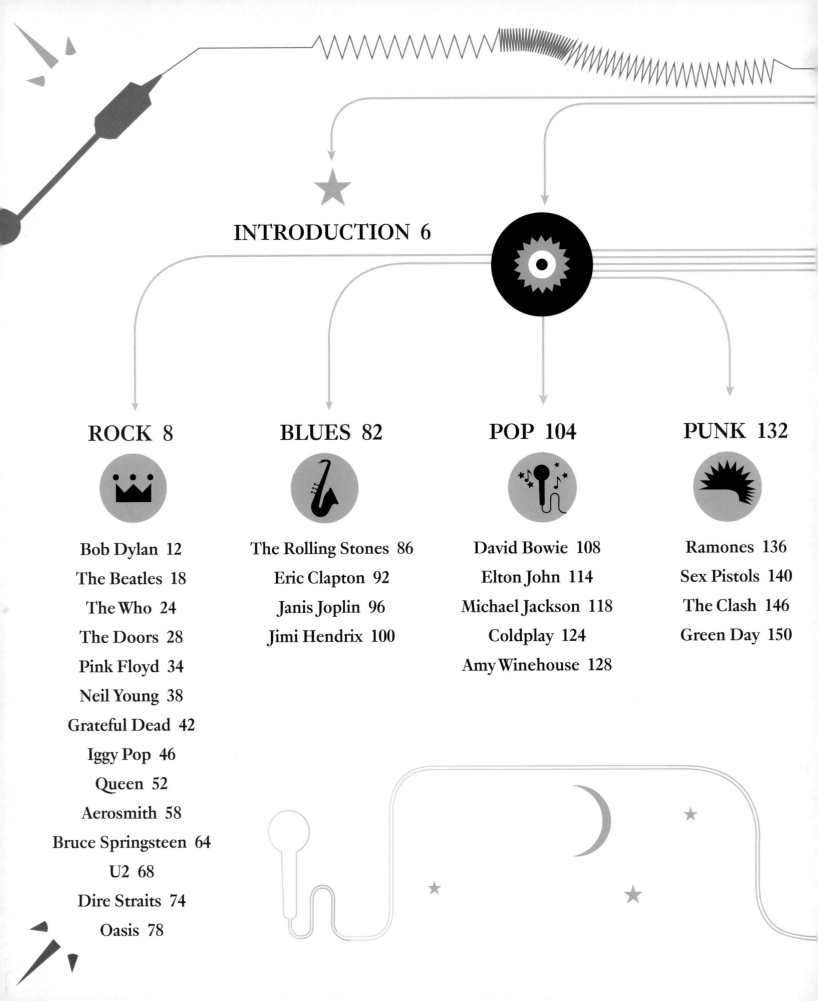

♪ Contents

Text **Ernesto Assante**
Infographics **Giulia De Amicis**

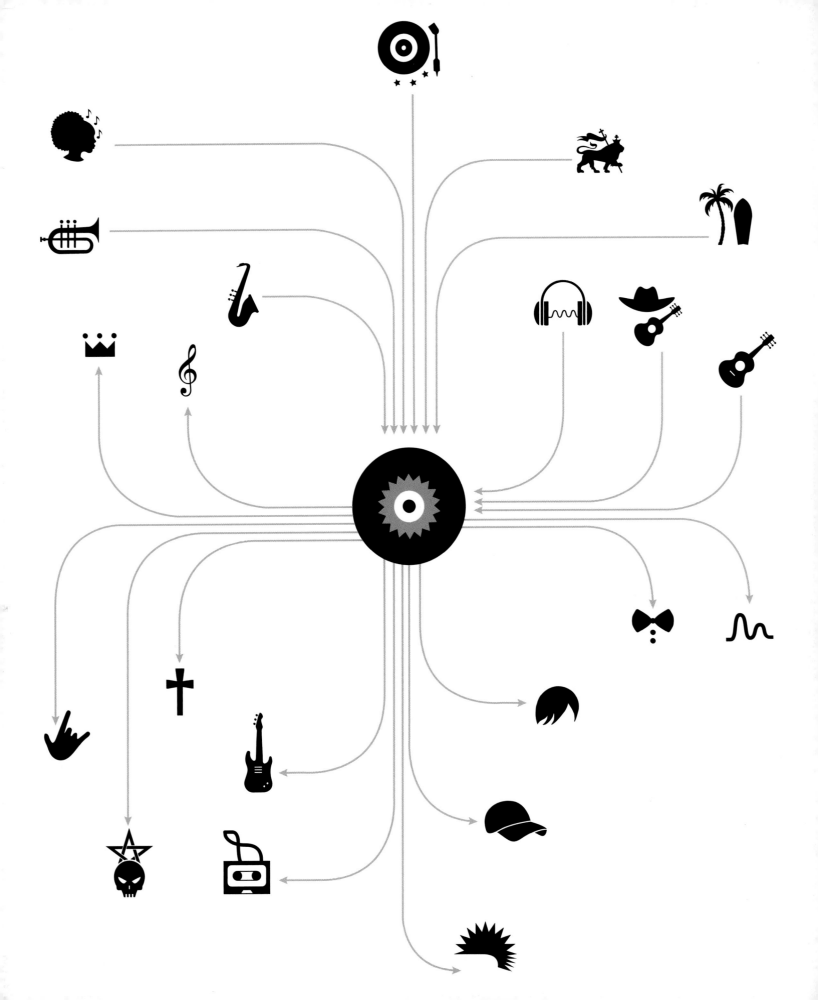

Introduction

Can the history of rock, or parts of it, be told through numbers and dates? One can certainly try. Numbers, with their simple clarity, tell us more than we may think, and at times they say it all. Even more so when it comes to numbers that reconstruct the passage of time, dates and events – anything and everything that qualifies as history. Likewise, the number of records sold and chart positions reveal the weight and substance of success while imparting a physical quality to something that is otherwise intangible. Here, numbers help draw a map; they trace the fundamental points of a period marked by transition and chart a course in a constantly flowing sea.

Infographics gather and combine forms of communication – information and data – and creative elements (those of graphic design) in order to visually represent what would otherwise be just numbers and texts. Infographics speak to us directly, immediately. They give a new visible shape to what numbers and words represent; they are a method, or better, a language that makes it possible to focus our attention on the information that is truly important. With that in mind, this book is an attempt to combine three things. First, the lyrics of rock songs and stories about the bands or written portraits of the artists; then photographs, images that offer a viewpoint and, to some degree, describe a kind of truth that goes beyond the sphere of music. Finally, and most importantly, infographics, the core of this volume, a new, different, colorful, and complete tool – 'musical', one might even say. A device that lets us tell the stories of rock and roll history in a different, rapid, immediate and captivating manner.

Narrating the history of rock through infographics is by no means an easy task. Certain elements integral to musical history cannot be reduced to graphics, numbers, and dates. However, infographics can help us avoid the aridity of numbers by concentrating on information, news and the curiosities that go well beyond a banal oversimplification to offer vantage points that may be both interesting and novel.

Rock

Try to imagine life without rock music. What kind of life would that be? What profound sadness would lurk in all the rocker hearts out there? Should rock disappear tomorrow, life would no longer make sense, not because aficionados would be unable to listen to other kinds of music, but because life would lose one of its most precious friends and champions. If what Springsteen says is true, that we were "born to run," we can do so only if we believe that the future will be better than the present, and that around every corner we may find not only a surprise but extraordinary emotions. This is exactly what the rock experience is all about. But it is essential that there be no confusion between 'us' and 'them'. 'They' listen to pop, content to dance mindlessly: those who still mistakenly think that a song cannot change someone's life. But we, we who love rock, know perfectly well that the next song might be the one that spurs us to take the next great leap forward, change direction, dream another dream. A song might inspire us to read a book or see a movie that we haven't heard of, discover a character or story worlds apart from us. At the very least, it will certainly change the course of the day itself.

How do you let the world know you are a true rocker? Well, there are the quintessential clothes, haircuts and attitudes, though they have also been adopted by those who have little or nothing to do with rock. Certainly, black boots are still useful, as is a leather jacket. Jeans and t-shirts are musts. But the clothes do not make the man. Third millennium rock cannot do without its music and an mp3 player or smartphone connected to the cloud stuffed in the pocket of an old pair of jeans.

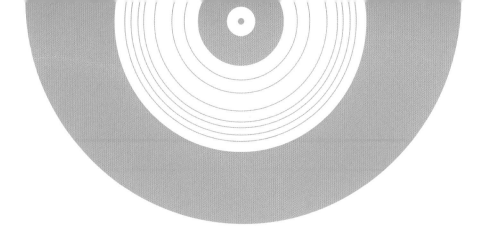

A shiny motorcycle or a vintage convertible are nice, but by no means a must. Whatever vehicle you've got, it absolutely cannot be without a stereo that can bring down the walls of Jericho when the Who's *Won't Get Fooled Again* comes on, or *The Pretender* by the Foo Fighters. In any case, there are no real rules concerning the clothes to wear, and perhaps there never have been. But up to the 1980s, it was de rigueur for rocker hairstyles to echo those of the bands and groups of the day. Now, however, genres and styles are so fluid, so 'mixed up', that extreme punk hairdos might crown the heads of dance music fans. What is certain is that hair should be long, but not too long, and ties, if worn at all, must absolutely be narrow.

One might be led to think that all this is the stuff of youths, since by definition rock has always been music for the rebellious young. This is true, but only in part: even after a certain age we can still be rockers 'inside' and forget about the 'outside'. Of course, by wearing 'normal' clothes and hairstyles, we're apparently like all the others; but our hearts definitely beat to a different rhythm. For those who were young in terms of calendar years up until recently, a rock lifestyle is still possible. It does not call for the obvious; instead, it prefers an element of surprise, a solid dose of non-stop head bangers at full blast. It loves company and friends (a.k.a. 'the band'), and consists of journeys as perfect 'citizens of the world' as well as evenings spent in live music venues.

It's worth noting that the rock lifestyle is not made up of nostalgia. Although the Beatles, Rolling Stones, Jimi Hendrix, Bob Dylan, the Doors, Cream and all the rest are an integral part of a rocker's daily diet, the true "prisoners of rock 'n' roll," as Springsteen said, listen to an endless bounty of new music and search daily for a feeling that's in sync with the times. And lest we forget, let's make it clear, especially to the older demographic, that true rockers never retire.

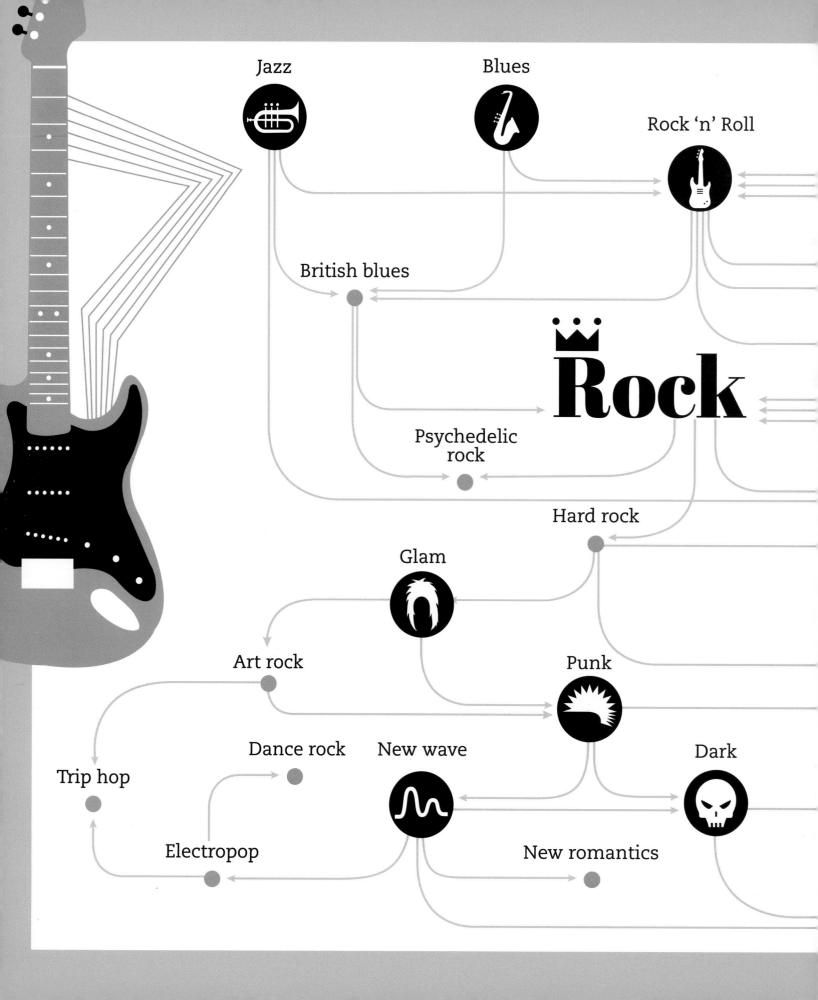

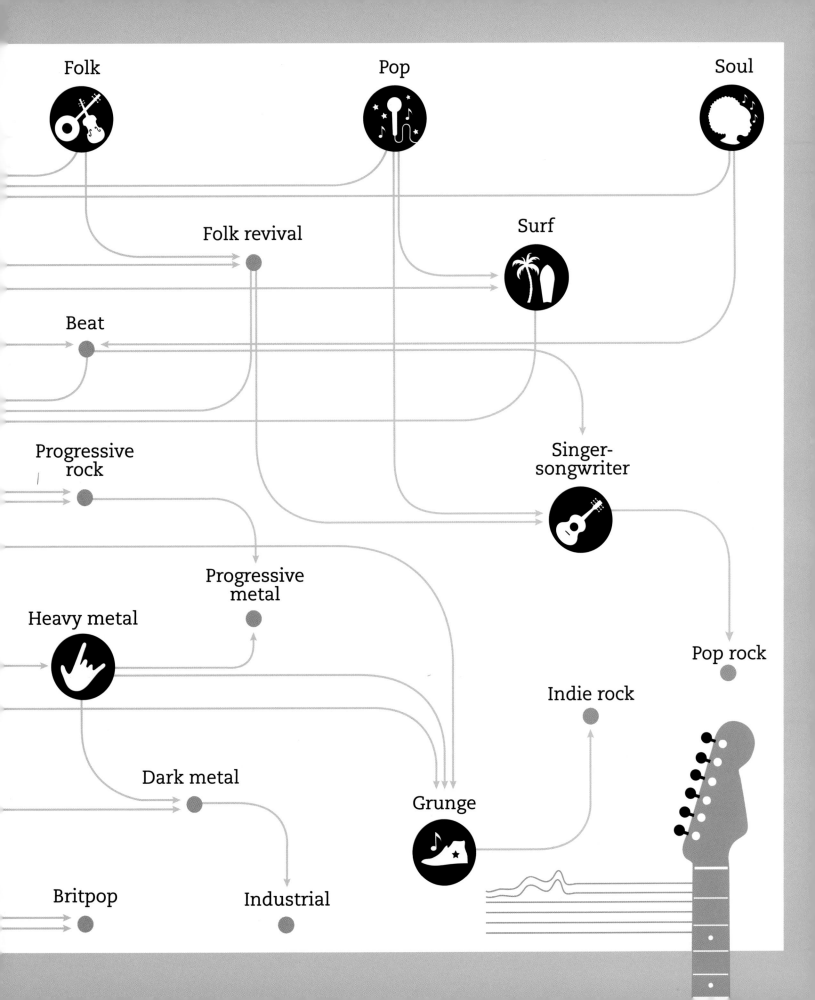

Bob **Dylan**

To love Bob Dylan's art is to love everything about him: his lyrics, the poetry of his songs, his music, the wonderful intertwining of what he says and how he says it, and, of course, his image and numerous personas.

Yet, incredible as it may seem considering how important and beloved he is, the resonance of his art in 20th-century cultural history, and his great popularity, relatively little is known about Dylan. All we have is the sparse information that he himself has provided, in different versions, in a handful of interviews, and his fragmentary autobiography. For over 50 years, people have spoken about and described Dylan, the man, with very few clues. Thanks to Jakob Dylan, the very image of the poet as a young man and frontman of the Wallflowers, we know that Bob has a son (he actually has six children, four of them with his first wife, Sara). Thanks to two biographies (*Down the Highway: the Life of Bob Dylan* by Howard Sounes, and Anthony Scaduto's legendary book, which has been updated several times), we know that up until 1992 Dylan had a second wife, Carol, who gave birth to Desireé (now 32), and that he is a deeply solitary person, obsessed with privacy. "He walks out there alone. He comes back off that stage alone. He writes those songs alone. He is his own man. He stands proud in his shoes. He don't need nobody to do nothin'," is what Carole Childs, a former girlfriend, had to say about Dylan. Her quote appears in Sounes's biography, a book that, despite shedding a bit of light on the Dylan mystery, is of course not authorized. Perhaps it's best to simply go with what Dylan himself had to say in his autobiography *Chronicles*, a spectacular example of musical literature and must-read for every music aficionado.

Listing his achievements in full would be impossible. Suffice it to say that his albums have sold over 100 million copies. He has won 11 Grammy Awards, one Golden Globe, and an Oscar. He received a special citation from the 2008 Pulitzer Prize jury "for his profound impact on popular music and American culture, marked by lyrical compositions of extraordinary poetic power," and the Presidential Medal of Freedom from Barack Obama in 2012. In 2016, he won the Nobel Prize for Literature "for having created new poetic expressions within the great American song tradition." The history of rock is long and, from Elvis in the 1950s to the present, many have written important works in this genre.

12-13 BOB DYLAN IN THE EARLY 1960S. DYLAN BEGAN HIS CAREER PLAYING IN CLUBS IN GREENWICH VILLAGE, NEW YORK CITY.

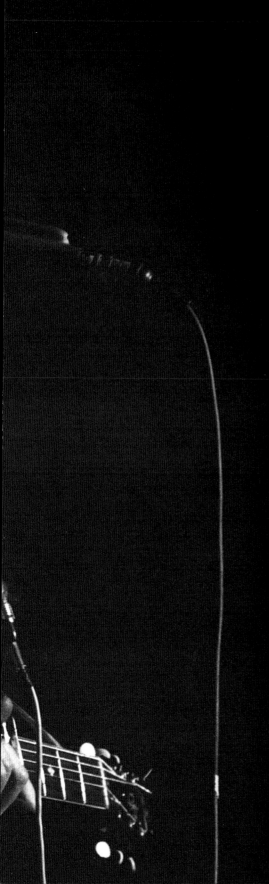

But no one has ever succeeded in doing what Dylan has done; no one has had, and maintained, the vitality, strength, originality and pride of Bob Dylan. More than 50 years of an active career have not lessened his fame and popularity. On the contrary, today Dylan seems to be enjoying one of the most interesting and successful phases of his long musical adventure. Once again, he has topped the charts, received one award after another, and is still influencing young generations of singer/songwriters everywhere. In short, Dylan has got his second (or even third) wind, again playing the role of the father of rock, while also demonstrating his capacity to narrate the musical present. His poetic voice has remained intact, his power as an interpreter has increased threefold, and his legendary elusiveness has become the norm. All this has made it possible for him to relate to younger generations of rock music fans, to collaborate with world-famous artists, write songs that sound both new and fresh, as well as familiar. In other words, he is the last punk songwriter and the first romantic one. Dylan is not an artist with nostalgia for the past, as his concerts attest, concerts in which he constantly reinterprets and revises his repertory to keep it relevant and vital to the present. He ensures that no dust settles on his old songs and that no rust corrodes even 'time-worn' classics, be they *Like a Rolling Stone* or *Mr. Tambourine Man*. Rock may change, new stars may have a better look or sell millions of discs, but Bob Dylan's albums remain evergreen, a must for those in search of great songwriting and splendid poetry.

14-15 BOB DYLAN ON STAGE DURING THE 1965 NEWPORT FESTIVAL, THE YEAR HE 'WENT ELECTRIC'.

Bob Dylan

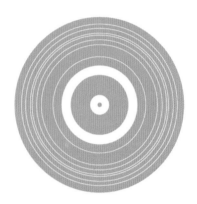

5,000
Number of copies of his
first album, released in 1962.

6,216
Number of times *Highway 61
Revisited* has been performed in
concert to date.

1941
Robert Allen
Zimmerman
(alias Bob Dylan)
is born in Duluth,
Minnesota.

1960
He drops his first
and last names
and becomes
Elston Gunn.

1963
Dylan and Joan
Baez sing at Martin
Luther King's *March
on Washington*.

1964
Dylan introduces
the Beatles to
marijuana.

1965
Dylan's 'electric
turning point' is
inaugurated at a
Newport Festival
concert.

6'09"
Runtime of *Like a Rolling Stone*, the
single that marked Dylan's 'electric
guitar turning point' in 1965.

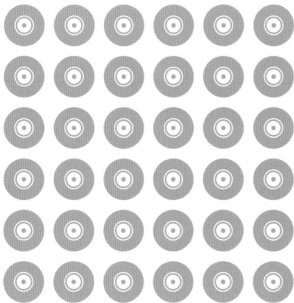

36

Studio albums recorded
to date.

8

Grammy Awards received.

1966

Dylan stops
performing live
after a motorcycle
accident.

1978

Dylan directs
the film *Renaldo &
Clara*.

1985

Dylan performs at
Live Aid with Keith
Richards and Ron
Wood.

1988

The Never Ending
Tour begins. By
2007 Dylan had
already played
2,000 concerts.

2016

Dylan wins the
Nobel Prize for
Literature (the first
rock musician to
receive this award).

3 +

No. of 'Christian period'
albums (1979-81: *Slow Train
Coming*, *Saved* and *Shot of Love*).

0

Times Dylan topped
the US singles charts.

The Beatles

Everyone knows about the Beatles. They are one of the pillars of contemporary popular culture despite the fact that their story ended almost 50 years ago. But their music is still very much with us, every day, in playlists, on the radio and television, and in films. The faces of the Fab Four are still an integral part of our collective imagination, eternally tied to their mop tops or long hair, colorful military uniforms or black boots, depending on the various phases of their stupendous musical adventure. They invented the 'beat'; together with Bob Dylan they were the founding fathers of rock as we know it today, and they wrote some of the most beautiful (and most famous) songs in the 20th century. They were part of the reason the world began to take notice of the younger generation, establishing new fashion rules, changing the mindset of an entire generation, and so on. And they did all this in less than ten years, essentially from 1962 to 1970, recording a dozen albums that have made history. At first, their formula was simple: a riff, a pleasant, easy-to-remember melodic line, essential instrumentation with bass, drums and two guitars – one rhythmic and one soloist – and, perhaps most importantly, no lead vocalist (and no leader), letting all four voices be heard. It was their team spirit that made the difference, the 'band' made up of youngsters who conveyed not only their music, but also their desire for a life based on a totally different set of rules from the past. But as they went on, their horizons broadened and they began to pave the way for rock, becoming fascinated with psychedelia, Indian influences and avant-garde music; they discovered and developed the extraordinary potential of recording studios, going on to become not only the most famous band in the world, but also the most important.

The Beatles reached their apex in the last three years of an astonishing career, beginning with the 1967 album, *Sgt. Pepper's Lonely Hearts Club Band*. It was something entirely new, a 'concept album' consisting of a series of songs connected to one another, abandoning the singles that had dominated the pop music scene and the record industry up until then. *The Beatles*, the extraordinary double album better known as the *White Album,* released in 1968, was a sort of collection of all the band's various souls and sonic explorations. Above all, it embodied the different personalities of the band, becoming one of the world's great 'pop patchworks', a record that to this day inspires a great many musicians, a combination of rock, psychedelia, avant-garde, melodic songwriting and pop. But it was in 1968 that the first signs of crisis and conflict emerged within the band, and two years later the Beatles disbanded for good. However, despite the tension and arguments among the four in 1969 and1970, they released two more albums: *Abbey Road* (1969), universally considered the band's last true record (an album that symbolically concludes with *The End*), and *Let It Be* (1970), which was actually recorded fifteen months before it was released.

John Lennon was murdered in New York by a mentally disturbed gunman in 1980, and George Harrison died in 2001 after a long illness. Paul and Ringo still tour, bringing with them the legend of a band from a small port town in England that changed the history of the world.

18   THE COVER OF *ABBEY ROAD*, DEPICTING THE FAB FOUR ON THE CROSSWALK IN FRONT OF EMI RECORDING STUDIOS.

THE BEATLES ★ ★ ★ ★

600

Beatles records, estimated in millions, sold up to today.

47.5

Millions of dollars Michael Jackson paid for the rights to the Beatles catalog in 1985.

2 🐦

Number of Beatles followers on Twitter, in millions.

29

The day in August 1966 of the last Beatles concert at Candlestick Park in San Francisco.

23

Consecutive weeks that *Hey Jude* stayed on the charts.

20

Singles that topped the US charts.

1962

The first of their 22 singles (plus 16 EPs) in their astonishing career was released: *Love Me Do*.

1964

The year the Beatles occupied the first five spots on the Billboard chart.

1966

The Beatles stop performing live.

1969

The year the rumor that Paul had died and was being replaced by a double, began to circulate.

129

Number of days needed to record *Sgt. Pepper*.

3,000

Estimated number of covers of *Yesterday* that have been recorded.

32

Songs written by Paul McCartney that topped the charts.

73

Number of people, in millions, who saw the Beatles' first TV appearance on the *Ed Sullivan Show* in 1964.

26

Songs written by John Lennon that hit no. 1 on the charts.

13

All Beatles albums recorded in their short career, plus Paul McCartney's first solo album, the three by John Lennon (two with Yoko Ono), George Harrison's three (including a triple album), and two by Ringo Starr, for a total (including double and triple albums) of 25 albums in only eight years.

THE BEATLES

7

Grammy Awards won by the Beatles.

7

Number of band names that the four considered before choosing the Beatles: Black Jacks, Quarrymen, Johnny and the Moondogs, Beatals, Long John and the Silver Beetles, Silver Beats, Silver Beatles.

1970

The Beatles disband.

The Beatles win an Oscar with *Let It Be*.

2017

Ringo Starr's last album, *Give More Love*, is released.

2018

Paul McCartney's last album, *Egypt Station*, is released.

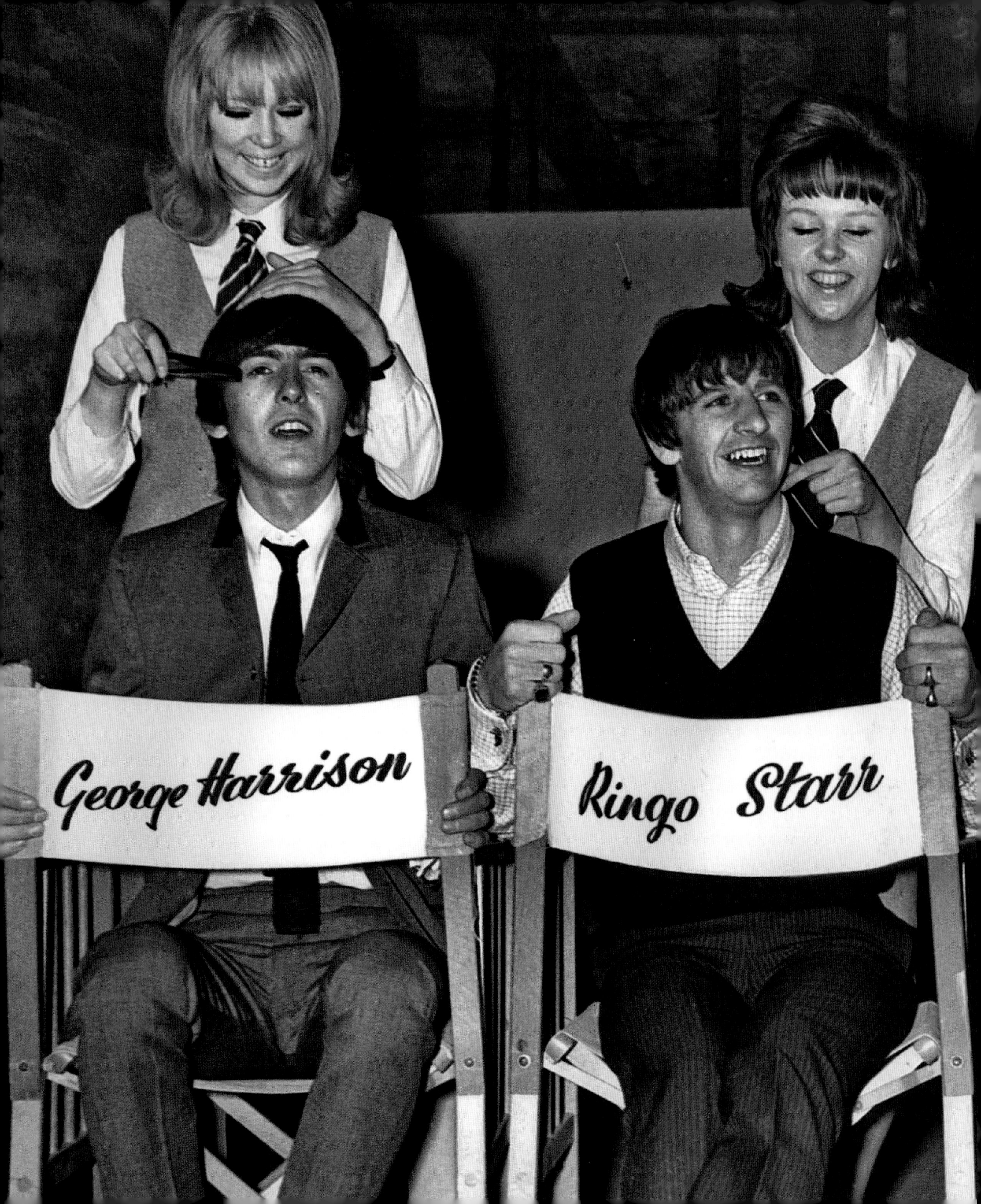
George Harrison
Ringo Starr

The Who

If you love rock you cannot but love the Who. Their music, written by Pete Townshend and performed on stage by the entire band (whose other members are Roger Daltrey, John Entwistle and Keith Moon) is a cornerstone of rock and its expressions, style and philosophy. Music simply would not be what it is today if, just over 50 years ago, Townshend hadn't started writing songs for Daltrey's voice.

Young, angry and electric, this creative group of Londoners didn't bother with good manners. To the contrary, their shows ended with the symbolic destruction of their instruments: four rockers in a world that moved at the speed of light and tried to change the rules of the game. They released their first album in 1965, the year when rock took on its definitive form: the Beatles abandoned beat and released *Help*, the Rolling Stones wrote *Satisfaction* and Dylan began to really rock, each of them contributing to the evolution of the genre. In *My Generation*, Townshend wrote caustic, spontaneous, direct lyrics: "People try to put us down / Just because we get around / Things they do look awful c-c-cold / I hope I die before I get old [...] / Why don't you all f-f-fade away / And don't try to dig what we all s-s-say / I'm not trying to cause a big s-s-sensation / I'm just talkin' 'bout my g-g-g-generation / This is my generation / This is my generation, baby." It was a massive boulder launched from a slingshot aimed at society. The electricity of Townshend's guitar, Entwistle's fast-paced bass, Moon's drumming and Daltrey's voice shattered the conventions of pop and released the anger of a generation that wanted to change the world. The Who became the poster band of the mods (modernists), a subculture of stylish, scooter-riding, parka-wearing, amphetamine-taking youths obsessed with rhythm 'n' blues, soul and ska. The Who spoke their language and while singing, Daltrey stuttered on purpose to underscore how difficult it was for youths to communicate with 'others' – adults and the world. This marked the beginning of the rock revolution, and Townshend's lyrics made the difference, becoming an integral part of the soundtrack of swinging London. What set the Who apart from other bands was the unbelievable musical power of the unique trio – Entwistle, Moon and Townshend – as well as their use of feedback, drumming that always seemed to be a solo, and bass that interacted so amazingly well with the guitar and percussion, all of which put the band in a class of its own. Such visionary creativity only further demonstrates that the band's ambition was not to produce lucrative singles, but to look forward, far ahead to the future. The result was *Tommy*, the world's first great rock opera, *Who's Next*, and *Quadrophenia*. The same holds true today, more than 50 years later, without Moon, who died in 1978, and Entwistle, who passed away in 2002: Pete Townshend and Roger Daltrey still perform with the same fantastic energy, regaling audiences with memorable songs and the power of rock music without equal.

24   THE WHO IN THE LATE 1960S. FROM LEFT: JOHN ENTWISTLE, ROGER DALTREY, PETE TOWNSHEND AND KEITH MOON.

The who

100

Number, in millions,
of albums sold.

1964

The band members
begin their career,
which is still in
progress.

1967

The year when, during the
Smothers Brothers Comedy Hour,
Keith Moon's drums exploded on
stage, causing Pete Townshend
to temporarily lose his hearing in
one ear.

1969

The year of
the historic
performance
at dawn during
Woodstock.

51
Albums
in the Who discography.

19
Number of movies vocalist
Roger Daltrey appeared in.

17
Albums that made the
English Top Ten.

10
Ranking given to Townshend
on the *Rolling Stone* 100 best
guitarists list.

2
Number of monumental rock
operas in double albums
that became movies: *Tommy*
(directed by Ken Russell)
and *Quadrophenia*
(directed by Franc Roddam).

2:
Original band
members
who are still alive.

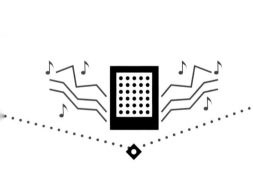

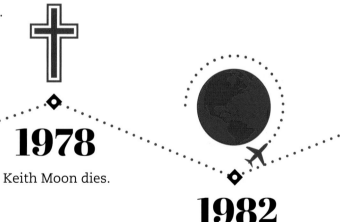

1978
Keith Moon dies.

2002
John Entwistle
dies.

1976
The Who perform at the
Charlton Athletic Football
Ground, a concert that, for ten
years, was in the Guinness
Book of Records as "the loudest
concert of all time."

1982
The Who's last tour
takes place.
The band is still active.

The Doors

Sometimes chance can change the course of history. It most certainly changed the history of rock when Jim Morrison met Ray Manzarek, one of the most legendary anecdotes of its kind. Manzarek and Morrison had finished their university studies a month earlier when, by chance, they met on the beach of Venice, in Los Angeles. Morrison told Manzarek that he wrote poetry and composed songs, and Manzarek said he wanted to take a listen. Among them was the first version of *Moonlight Drive*, thoroughly appreciated by Manzarek. When the two decided to form the Doors, once again it was chance – or rather, the transcendental meditation of Maharishi (the same guru admired by the Beatles) – that led Manzarek to find the other two members of the band, John Densmore and Robbie Krieger, at a meditation session. Once the fate of the four had been sealed in a rather singular band consisting of a keyboardist, guitarist, drummer and vocalist (no bassist), rock and poetry were combined in a highly original manner. Morrison was an electrifying shaman, a poet in search of beauty, an incredible and magnetic stage performer who mesmerized anyone within earshot. The other three members went along with the Lizard King, giving full rein

to their creativity in interminably long and demanding improvisations, mixing their great love for blues with rock, jazz, and even classical.

The band's beginnings were marked by unsuccessful performances in small, half-empty clubs in Los Angeles, but evening after evening the band grew and honed their potential. Morrison became increasingly audacious and sure of himself, Densmore and Krieger succeeded in transforming blues into incandescent creative material, and Manzarek – the 'architect' – made everything they did excitingly new, different, psychedelic and romantic. After being hired as the house band at the Whisky a Go Go in LA, the Who landed their first contract with Columbia. Then, signing a much more interesting deal with Elektra Records, the band released its first album, *The Doors*, in 1967 – much of the success of which was due to the legendary single *Light my Fire*.

The sound of Manzarek's organ, a Vox, flanked by an electric keyboard used mostly for the bassline, was the unmistakable trademark of the Los Angeles band, the perfect platform from which to launch Morrison's voice, vocal improvisations, and raging, romantic, poetic and incendiary interpretations.

28   JIM MORRISON, SINGER, POET AND FRONTMAN OF THE DOORS, WHO DIED IN 1971 IN PARIS.

the doors

The rich musical vocabulary of Manzarek, Krieger and Densmore also had a role to play in taking the band beyond the confines of blues into various, wide-randing territories that were both more pop and openly experimental. A short career, great success, overwhelming concerts, problems with the law and 'the Man', the pleasure of rebellion and the dream of revolution ("We want the world and we want it now") turned the Doors and Morrison into a legend, one made of desire, passion and poetry.

30-31 THE DOORS POSING DURING A PHOTO SHOOT. FROM LEFT: JIM MORRISON, JOHN DENSMORE, RAY MANZAREK AND ROBBIE KRIEGER.

THE doors

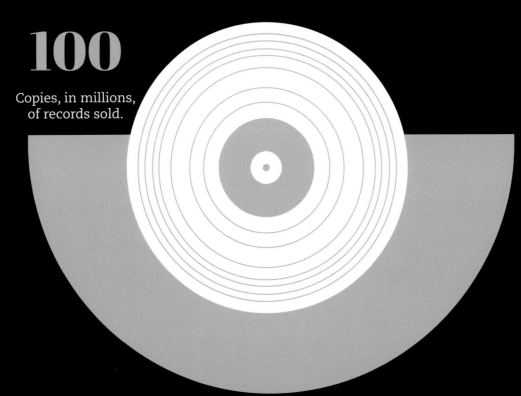

100

Copies, in millions,
of records sold.

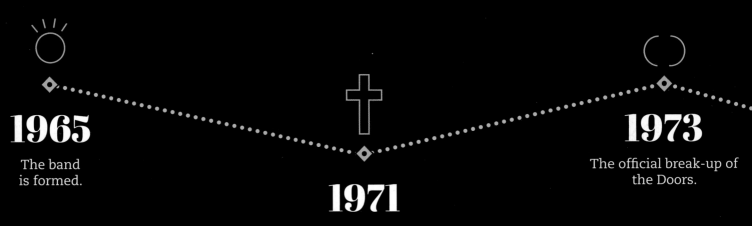

1965

The band
is formed.

1971

Jim Morrison
dies in Paris.

1973

The official break-up of
the Doors.

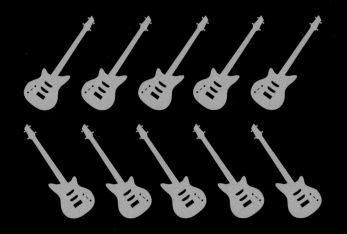

10

Number of bassists who collaborated on the recordings and tours of the band, which never had a permanent bassist.

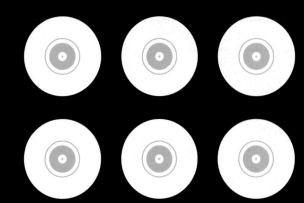

6

Studio albums recorded by all four members of the band.

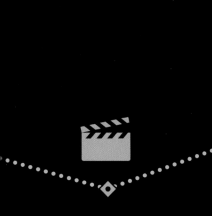

1993

The band is inducted into the Rock and Roll Hall of Fame.

1991

Oliver Stone's film *The Doors* is released, with Val Kilmer in the role of Jim Morrison and Kyle MacLachlan (FBI agent Cooper in *Twin Peaks*) as Ray Manzarek.

2002

Ray Manzarek and Robby Krieger form the Doors of the 21st Century with Ian Astbury of the Cult as vocalist, Angelo Barbera as bassist and drummer Stewart Copeland of the Police.

2007

The Doors get a star on the Hollywood Walk of Fame at 6901 Hollywood Boulevard.

THE DOORS

Pink Floyd

Can you live without Pink Floyd? Probably yes, but life will certainly be the worse for it. The band's music and art speaks to us; it tells us about ourselves. More than any other group in contemporary 'popular' music, Roger Waters, David Gilmour, Rick Wright and Nick Mason have delved into the themes of human existence and, thanks to their insight, they have forever influenced the collective imagination through immortal works that are still topical and moving today.

We can no longer see Pink Floyd perform live, but we can listen to their music – the solo concerts and tours of Roger Waters and, in particular, the albums they recorded during the band's extraordinary career. Listening to them is a headlong dive into a multi-sensory experience that takes us on a journey through time, from the very beginning to the present. It's a trip consisting of various fascinating hypotheses and projects that combine past and the future, Pompeii and the Battersea Power Station, psychedelia and war, London's beat music scene and Thatcher's England, lost among the unique covers designed by Hipgnosis or amid the sounds of their concerts. Those discs contain everything Pink Floyd has done, everything that has made them such an important part of 20th-century – and even contemporary – culture.

More than fifty years ago, in March 1967, Pink Floyd released its first single, *Arnold Layne*. Those fifty years have borne witness to contemporary music masterpieces: *Atom Heart Mother, Ummagumma, Dark Side of the Moon, The Wall*. Years in which the band revolutionized the very way we think of concerts, produced exceptional visual innovations, used every technological device they could get their hands on, and established new rules for contemporary art.

If course, it all began with Syd Barrett, the genie who escaped the lamp and went on to lead the band in its initial, fundamental phase, followed by the arrival of Gilmour. Then came the period of Waters' grand compositional and theatrical visions, followed by the one in which Gilmour and Mason led the band, an era that only ended a few years ago. Our world owes much to Pink Floyd's inventiveness, contemporary music owes much more, and the 20th century even more. The band opened doors, passed over frontiers, invented worlds, combined the obvious and the sublime, pop and avant-garde, electronica and ballads, paired with Barrett's astral creations, Gilmour's undisputedly unique guitar style, Mason's sophisticated and precise drumming style, and the amazing intuition of Waters and Wright's subtle elegance. *Dark Side of the Moon* and *The Wall* are and will always be masterpieces without which it would be difficult even to grasp what rock has been, and what it might still become.

34   THE MEMBERS OF PINK FLOYD WRAPPED IN PINK CLOTH. FROM LEFT: NICK MASON, DAVID GILMOUR AND RICK WRIGHT; BELOW THEM, ROGER WATERS.

Pink Floyd

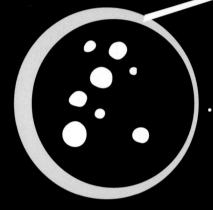

15

Number of studio albums in the Pink Floyd discography, which also includes 4 live albums, 12 compilations and 26 singles recorded in a period lasting almost 40 years.

50

Copies sold, in millions, of *The Dark Side of the Moon*, making it the third best-selling album of all time.

1965

Year of the London formation of the band, which, after making its debut as The Tea Set, adopted the name of two bluesmen, Pink Anderson and Floyd Council.

1968

Stanley Kubrick refuses Pink Floyd's proposal to record the soundtrack of 2001: *Space Odyssey* and also discards Alex North's music, deciding to use only already edited classical music.

1970

Revenge: Roger Waters does not allow Kubrick to use part of his *Atom Heart Mother* suite in the soundtrack of *Clockwork Orange*.

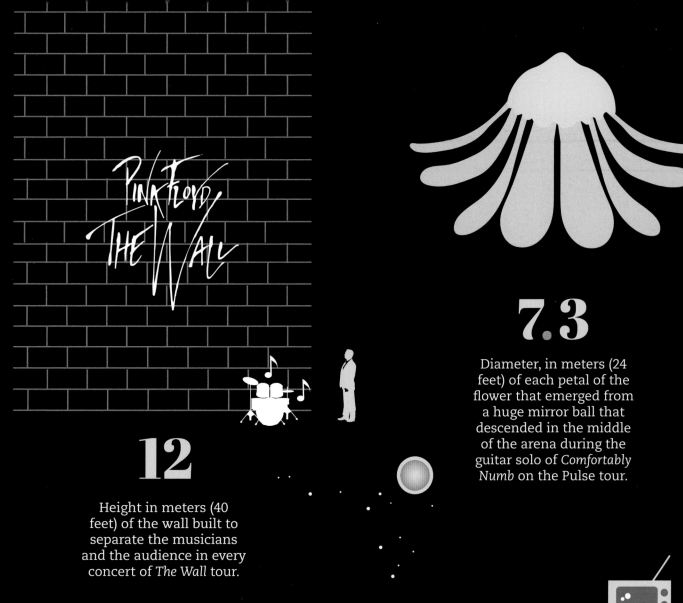

7.3

Diameter, in meters (24 feet) of each petal of the flower that emerged from a huge mirror ball that descended in the middle of the arena during the guitar solo of *Comfortably Numb* on the Pulse tour.

12

Height in meters (40 feet) of the wall built to separate the musicians and the audience in every concert of *The Wall* tour.

1970

That same year, Pink Floyd's music is used in another epoch-defining film: Antonioni's *Zabriskie Point*.

1971

Pink Floyd members star in the concert film *Pink Floyd: Live at Pompeii*, directed by Adrian Maben and set in the Roman amphitheater of Pompeii.

1989

Another concert in a unique setting: during the *A Momentary Lapse of Reason* tour, Pink Floyd performs on a floating stage in St. Mark's Lagoon in Venice, broadcast around the world.

Neil Young

You've got Elvis, the Beatles, Dylan, the Stones, punk, electronica, country, psychedelia, grunge and new wave – and rock, which has changed, died and been reborn several times. From 1966 to the present, the only person who has been right there with all its ups and downs, who has expressed and experienced the various changes in youth culture, and who has tried desperately and intelligently to lend meaning and sense to both the words and sound of rock, is Neil Young.

The poet-singer of desperation and joy, both adventurous and solitary, Neil Young has plunged into the depths of music more than just about anyone else. He is both a singer-songwriter and musician, an experimenter and traditionalist; he has combined the best and worst of youth culture, in all its terrible defeats and sensational victories. So it is no coincidence that younger generations, the latest wave of rockers, consider him the only 'dinosaur' from the 1960s who deserves citizenship in the present-day rock nation. And they're right. For Young, rock is closely bonded to life and sentiments, infusing the extraordinary, piercing sound of his guitar with the secrets of 50 years worth of youth music history, and maybe even the secrets of tomorrow's.

Today you could very well get by without listening to his new albums, but if you really love rock, you can't miss one of his concerts. Like a Springsteen concert, Neil Young on stage is living proof that rock is an idea and a language, but also proof of the communicative power of a form of music that, when authentic, is never predictable or repetitive.

Young improvises with his long, shattering electric guitar solos, like a jazz musician searching for a definitive note. Every piece is expanded, disassembled and reconstructed, and at times even the lyrics undergo the same process. Like a preacher, Neil speaks of peace, love, struggle, commitment and rebellion; his songs are against war, the destruction of the planet, and greed, and all for love, as they have always been. And frankly, one note alone - perhaps played to the breaking point, amplified and distorted, sculpted with the amazingly vibrant sound that his guitar expresses – is enough to make Neil Young a rock music legend. He is one of the greatest guitarists of all time, informal, surprising and eclectic, Hendrixian to the nth degree. And yet, he also possesses a unique style in which technique gives way to sudden, spontaneous creation, going straight to the heart, eschewing 'tricks'. For that matter, Young himself is like his sound, with his 'hard' hippie air, his dark glasses and motorcycle, and his personal life marked by continuous ups and downs, surges and descents into darkness. Young wrote his story just as he wanted: first with Buffalo Springfield, then with the super band formed with David Crosby, Stephen Stills and Graham Nash and the endless turnabouts of their reunions, fights, and interwoven collaborations. Then there are his innumerable solo discs, some of which are historic, others connected to current events and politics, and yet others adapted to his mood. The fact is, Neil Young is still the solitary hero of rock 'n' roll, a man who roves the world, guitar in hand, without ever stopping.

CANADIAN SINGER-SONGWRITER AND GUITARIST NEIL YOUNG PERFORMING DURING A LIVE CONCERT.

Neil Young

14.3

Copies sold, in millions, of *Déjà Vu*, the first album from Crosby, Stills, Nash & Young (1970). It was a worldwide success at the time, even greater than that enjoyed by the Beatles albums released after they disbanded.

3

Dollars, in millions, invested by Neil Young personally in the production of the film *Human Highway* (from the title of a song in the album *Comes a Time*).

1,500

Number of acres of Young's Broken Arrow ranch in La Honda, California.

44

Years that have passed without a CD re-release of the album *Time Fades Away*, which consisted of new songs, recorded live in 1973, making it the 'least popular' of Neil Young's releases.

1953

The year of the model of his most famous electric guitar, the Gibson Les Paul Goldtop, renamed Old Black because of the black varnish on the original.

1958

The year Young was given his first musical instrument, a plastic ukulele.

1963

The first single of the Squires, Young's first band, is released

36

Years Young was married to Pegi Young (née Morton), who died in 2019.

35

The playing time, in minutes, of *Arc*, the 'craziest' of Neil Young's many absurd albums, which consists only of fragments of guitar feedback recorded during his 1991 tour with Crazy Horse.

30

The number of books written by his father, the journalist and author Scott Young.

6

The musicians who were members of Crazy Horse, the band most associated with Neil Young. Besides the band's most recent members (Billy Talbot, Ralph Molina and Nils Lofgren), the other, 'authentic' Crazy Horses are the late Danny Whitten and Jack Nietzsche, and the recently-retired Frank Poncho Sampedro.

30

The songs by Young which mention the moon.

102.2

Degrees Fahrenheit (39° Celsius) of the fever Young had the day he composed, while in bed, four songs that he later recorded for his second album (1969): *Everybody Knows This Is Nowhere*, *Cinnamon Girl*, *Cowgirl in the Sand* and *Down by the River*.

3

Movies Young has co-directed: *Journey Through the Past, Rust Never Sleeps* and *Human Highway*.

1972

Neil Young is at the apex of his career: *Harvest* is the best-selling album in the United States, and the single *Heart of Gold* is at the top of the charts.

2009

The first Neil Young Archives volume is released (8 CDs covering the years from 1963 to 1972).

Grateful Dead

June 1967 was an important month for the Grateful Dead. The band's first album had been released a few weeks earlier and on June 18 it would perform at the first great rock festival in history, the Monterey Pop Festival. An overwhelming beginning for a group that had made a major contribution not only to the history of rock, but to the history of 20th-century culture in general. Bob Weir, Jerry Garcia, Phil Lesh, Bill Kreutzmann, Ron 'Pigpen' McKernan and Mickey Hart were the line-up that animated Ken Kesey's Acid Tests, transforming concerts into events for thousands of fans, and leading rock into the heart of psychedelia in an attempt to go "where no human being had ever been before", musically speaking. The Grateful Dead was more than a group; it was its own planet populated by millions of devoted fans. It was cultural currency, a lifestyle that to this day continues to influence younger generations, as Martin Scorsese has pointed out. The band's artistic, creative and personal story was marvelous and unique from the beginning, connected to traditional American music, to the hippie turning point in San Francisco and up to the end of their adventure in 1995, after the death of Jerry Garcia. But the Grateful Dead is anything but dead, and to this day its music continues to influence a large number of other bands and inspires legions of fans to dream. Current events and history were always at the heart of the legendary California jam band which, 50 years ago, paved the way for psychedelic rock, roaming the streets of San Francisco, often side by side with Ken Kesey's Merry Pranksters during their 'acid test events',

experimenting with the limits of perception through LSD trips, and the limits of music by taking a cue from blues and rock. Jerry Garcia was the soul of the band: guitarist, composer, and the reluctant counterculture star of a generation who dreamed of a new, different world. An astonishingly gifted guitarist who grew out of folk and blues traditions, a passionate researcher and tireless experimenter, Garcia was the very heart and soul of the Grateful Dead, which he led up the end of the 20th century without ever losing the way on what can only be described as a long strange trip.

Various generations of fans grew up with the band, and those in America morphed into a real community, the Deadheads, with unique rituals, rules, clothing and means of transportation. The latter allowed them to follow the band, taking to the road during its tours, concert after concert: a caravan traveling the length and breadth of the United States, sowing 'good vibes' and great music everywhere.

The Grateful Dead are not only an important element for rock and American music overall, but a fundamental part of the very history of the United States. Having left a lasting mark on the 1960s and 1970s, for many, the band is still an integral part of the American Dream, precisely because it kept on truckin' forward. It represented the American idea of freedom, touring the States with a large 'family' whose motto was, more or less: you can join us if you want, you can go off if you want; we don't know what will happen but what we do know is that we'll never look back.

42 NEW YORK, 1972: THE GRATEFUL DEAD IN A JAM SESSION WITH ANOTHER GREAT AMERICAN GROUP, THE ALLMAN BROTHERS BAND.

GRATEFUL DEAD

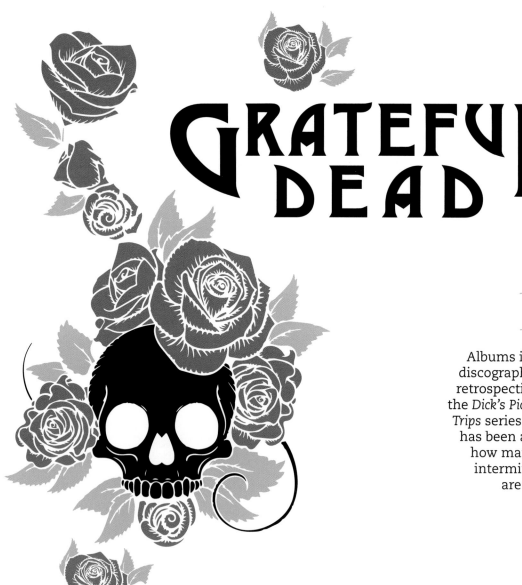

175

Albums in the Grateful Dead discography, also including live retrospective performances and the *Dick's Picks*, *Dave Picks* and *Road Trips* series. To date, no computer has been able to even estimate how many bootlegs of their interminable live concerts are in circulation.

32

Albums in their career: 13 studio recordings, 10 live recordings and 9 compilations.

1946

At only four years old, Jerry Garcia (1942-1995) loses the middle finger on his right hand when his brother Clifford accidentally cut it off with an ax while chopping firewood. This accident didn't stop him from becoming one of the most legendary guitarists in the history of rock.

1965

The Grateful Dead is formed in the San Francisco Bay Area.

10,000

Live Grateful Dead recordings available on the Internet Archive.

2,318

Number of concerts in which Jerry Garcia played during his 30-year career.

100

Versions of the song *Black Star* compiled by John Oswald in the album *Grayfolded*.

45

Number of albums that Jerry Garcia recorded with the Grateful Dead, as well as the number of his live solo albums.

30

Minimum number of minutes that *Black Star* – a single with a duration of 2'10", released in 1967 and received coolly – lasted in live performances, becoming a 'trademark' of the Grateful Dead.

13

Number of musicians that appeared on stage under the Grateful Dead skull and roses logo.

1995

Jerry Garcia dies.

Iggy Pop

He recently turned seventy, but he could very well be half that age. Or double, depending on how you look at it, since it seems that Iggy Pop has always been part of the rock scene. He was hidden in the pelvis of Elvis when the latter did his first rock 'n' roll 'bump and grind' in Memphis. He was between the lips of Mick Jagger when he flirted with the devil, and was part of John Lydon's furious smirk as he shouted "No future." Iggy was really with Bowie when he spoke about his licentious *joie de vivre,* and with The Stooges when they brought down the walls of Jericho with the terrific sound of their electric guitars. And he will also be among the strings of the guitar of a beardless boy working on his next song of love and rage in a cellar god knows where. Further still, he is inside all of us when we grow tired of the usual routine and want something else: more life, more passion, more rebellion, more dreams and more love, sex and rock 'n' roll. Yes, Iggy Pop is inside each of us, but while we keep our demons hidden, he personifies them, puts them on stage, throws them in our faces as he leaps onto the stage of life stripped to the waist.

It was in 1965 that James Newell Osterberg discovered he was Iguana Pop. He had already been playing with bands in the Detroit area for two years, getting his start as a drummer, when he realized that remaining seated on a stool was not for him. It was also in 1965 that, together with the Asheton brothers and Dave Alexander, he formed the Psychedelic Stooges band, which exactly 50 years ago became The Stooges, and tried to reshuffle rock. They did this with three albums that many people consider the ABCs of hard, brazen rock, the alphabet of the punk that was to come, the bible of electric nirvana: *The Stooges* (1969), *Fun House* (1970) and *Raw Power* (1973), which were more than enough to become legendary. Yet this wasn't enough for Iggy, who, through excesses and drug abuse, was heading rapidly toward self-destruction, taking every curve of life at a breakneck speed. It was David Bowie who, before the release of *Raw Power*, first tried to save Iggy's life and career. But only in 1976, when Bowie took him to Berlin, did he finally succeeded in saving him. And in the following year alone, Iggy recorded two overwhelming albums, *The Idiot* and *Lust for Life*, true masterpieces, LPs in which his personality took on definitive shape. Not only that, but Bowie managed to get his friend to channel his overwhelming energy toward creativity, realizing such fundamental songs as *Fun Time, Nightclubbing, Lust for Life, The Passenger,* and *China Girl.*

Iggy Pop, the man and myth was consolidated over the following years, with concerts that were increasingly explosive and albums made of flesh and blood, melodies and electricity, producing songs such as *Real Wild Child* and discs like *American Caesar,* not to mention the endless list of collaborations, projects, films and documentaries, TV shows, soundtracks, surprising duets, and so much more.

46 IGGY POP, THE FOUNDER OF THE STOOGES, JOKINGLY POSING WITH A CIGARETTE IN HIS NOSE (FEBRUARY 1970).

47

He did all this only out of his inordinate love of music and life, out of his sheer delight in surprising others and even himself. Iggy is an extraordinary performer, following in the footsteps of Elvis and Jim Morrison, a model for rock singers everywhere, the symbol of music channeled into vital energy that today, it must be said, seems to have few followers. Listen to him once again, go to his concerts: it will surely be a unique experience, especially for those who have never seen him perform live, have never been overwhelmed by that incredible mixture of energy, madness, poetry and life that only Iggy Pop knows how to embody on stage.

48-49   IGGY POP AMID HIS FANS DURING A CONCERT AT CROSLEY FIELD IN CINCINNA-TI, OHIO IN JUNE 1970.

49   THE STOOGES BACKSTAGE AT THE WHISKY A GO GO (LOS ANGELES, 1973). FROM LEFT, STANDING, ARE SCOTT THURSTON, RON ASHETON AND JAMES WILLIAMSON; SEATED, IGGY POP AND SCOTT ASHETON.

IGGY POP

20

Number of other musicians' albums on which Iggy has collaborated: from Slash and Rob Zombie to the 'unpredictable' Ryūichi Sakamoto and Ofra Haza, up to Kesha.

3

Number of records that have become part of the history of extremely noisy rock: *The Stooges* (1969), *Funhouse* (1970) and *Raw Power* (1973).

3

Number of bands with which Iggy Pop has played: The Iguanas (the origin of Iggy's nom de plume), The Psychedelic Stooges, and The Stooges.

1970

During a legendary concert at Ungano's in New York, Iggy pulls his penis out of his trousers and sets it on an amplifier.

1947

James Newell Osterberg, the future Iggy Pop, is born on April 21 in Muskegon, Michigan.

18

Number of movies Iggy has acted in, beginning in 1986 with Alex Cox's *Sid & Nancy*, on the life of Sid Vicious and the Sex Pistols.

6

Genres in which Iggy excelled: garage rock, hard rock, heavy metal, glam rock, punk and noise.

4

Discs he produced with his friend David Bowie: *Raw Power, The Idiot, Lust for Life,* and *Blah Blah Blah.*

2

Number of David Bowie albums in which Iggy took part as a backing vocalist: *Low* (1977) and *Tonight* (1984).

1

Number of Zucchero albums on which Iggy Pop collaborated: *Chocabeck.*

2011

Photographer Mikael Jansson documents Iggy's debut in a fashion magazine wearing a cocktail dress and a Dior handbag.

1977

David Bowie is only the backup keyboard accompanist during Iggy's world tour.

Queen

From nine to ninety, everyone and their mother loves Queen, from elementary school kids to retired grandparents. Queen is one of the very few bands that is not subject to the ravages of time, not peremptorily declared 'old' by those under 25 and not 'skipped' on veteran rock fans' playlists, where they always seem to appear between a track by the Rolling Stones and one by AC/DC. Queen, together with Pink Floyd and the Beatles, have joined the pantheon of eternal rock bands enjoyed even by hip hop fans and metalheads. Today's generation gap - so clearly visible on the charts, totally dominated by rap and trap while other genres are totally lacking - does not exist as far as Queen are concerned. Brian May explains why: "At a certain point in our career we no longer played for the public, but with the public." So, everyone's invited to Queen's parties, the door is open, there's room for one and all. Consequently, besides having invented the genre of operatic rock, the apotheosis of which is the single that almost everyone on the globe knows by heart, *Bohemian Rhapsody*, Queen did just that, they "played with the public," experimenting with rock and glam, pop and gospel, dance and electropop, and obviously also drawing from David Bowie, while eluding categorization, labels and stagnation. Nothing was ever immobile in Queen's musical universe, which makes it ideal for its admirers and fans today. So, in a world of streamed music, which makes everything 'contemporary', there is a song by Queen for all tastes, for those who are desperately in love, those who dream of a different life, those was want to clap their hands on time and those who want to dance, for those who adore the mixture of high brow and popular music, and those who, on the other hand, are quite content with a simple three-note riff. The only genre lacking is hip hop, but only because Mercury didn't have the time to lead his band in that direction.

And then there's an aspect that mustn't be underestimated: the extraordinary character of Freddie Mercury, the frontman, vocalist and driving force of the band. Mercury was not a singer like all others; he was a dazzling theatrical rock star, a brazen and captivating performer able to astonish the public and, obviously, sing like very few others in the world. His life reads like a novel, portrayed in the sensationally successful, multiple award-winning film *Bohemian Rhapsody*. It is the tale of the birth of a hero, his rise, fall and heroic recovery and triumph - an unbeatable story, especially if the hero wears leggings, has a voice so special it can be both epic and excruciating, and, especially, if it ends on a high note. Because after all, *Bohemian Rhapsody* ends in the most beautiful way possible: the Live Aid concert in 1985. So this fairy tale gets its happy ending too: Mercury does not die in the film, and perhaps, in some way, he's still here singing along with us.

QUEEN IN A FRAME OF THE BOHEMIAN RHAPSODY VIDEO. CLOCKWISE FROM LEFT, ROGER TAYLOR, BRIAN MAY, JOHN DEACON AND FREDDIE MERCURY.

The proof is in the crowds who flocked movie theaters, not to see a hero fall and be forgotten, an old rock star nearing retirement, or a celebrity who has faded into obscurity, but rather a star that still shines brightly, a brilliant presence no one seems able to do without.

There's no need to be nostalgic, because Freddie Mercury is alive, with his music and songs, his band and excesses, his love stories and flaws. And the magic of his performances has ensured that he will never die.

54   QUEEN, FREDDIE MERCURY'S LEGENDARY BAND, PLAYING IN MADISON SQUARE GARDEN, NEW YORK IN 1977.

55   FREDDIE MERCURY'S LAST CONCERT WITH QUEEN, AT KNEBWORTH IN 1986.

QUEEN

300

Copies, in millions, of albums Queen has sold to this day.

3,000

The minimum amount of pounds sterling needed to purchase one of the 200 numbered copies of the special edition of the *Bohemian Rhapsody* vinyl 45 with a maroon cover and gold letters.

707

Number of live concerts with Queen's original members.

1946

Farrokh Bulsara is born in the Government Hospital of Stone Town, the oldest section of Zanzibar City, Zanzibar. But the whole world knows him as Freddie Mercury.

1970

The band is formed.

26

Countries in which the band has performed.

24

The day in November 1991 when Freddie died, one day after publicly announcing he had AIDS.

15

The number of the quartet's studio albums.

6

The sixpence coin that Brian May used instead of a pick to play the guitar.

1

Freddie Mercury's position on the *Classic Rock* list of the best singers of all time.

17473

The asteroid discovered in 1991 (the year of Mercury's death), which was renamed 17473 Freddiemercury in his honor.

4

The zodiac signs of the band members on the Queen logo designed by Mercury: two lions for Leo (John Deacon and Roger Taylor), a crab for Cancer (Brian May) and two fairies for Virgo (Freddie Mercury). The signs surround the letter Q with a crown inside and a phoenix above.

1981

Greatest Hits is released, the best-selling album of all time in England.

1985

Queen plays the triumphant Live Aid concert.

1991

The year (on November 23) Mercury admits he has AIDS.

Aerosmith

Hailing from Boston, having begun their musical career in the 1970s, now, more than 40 years later, they are still one of the greatest rock bands of all time. The story of Aerosmith is simple and clear, consisting of fine songs and great prowess interpreting rock in a straightforward manner and therefore in blending their sound with that of the period they live in. A rock, hard rock and rock pop band, Aerosmith can play everything, and do so better than most. Formed in 1970, Aerosmith made its recording debut in 1973, but it was the third album, *Toys in the Attic*, released in 1975, that turned its members into true stars, following in the wake of the Rolling Stones while retaining their own distinct personality and sound. Aerosmith has had several lives, has been 'born' and has 'died' again and again. It has known periods of sensational success, like in the 1990s when *Get a Grip* sold more than 20 million copies and when the single *I Don't Wanna Miss a Thing* (the soundtrack of the movie *Armageddon*) topped the charts in half the world. Naturally, the band has also had its periods of deep crisis, such as in late 1979, when guitarist Joe Perry and vocalist Steven Tyler got into a furious argument. Perry quit the band and it seemed the group would not be able to get back on course, but the 'toxic twins' (Tyler and Perry) are, deep down, really good friends, as well as the very heart of Aerosmith. As its main songwriters (they've written almost 100 tracks together), they are indestructible and overwhelming, the classic example of rock 'n' roll friendship. And, as is common among friends, besides arguing they know how to make up, which is precisely what happened in 1984, when the band revived its original lineup. Excessive, spectacular, passionate, Tyler and Perry alone occupy almost the entire stage; in fact, the other three band members – Brad Whitford, Tom Hamilton and Joey Kramer – are known as the LI3 (Less Important 3). But this is neither here nor there, because Aerosmith, like every self-respecting band, is a well-knit team able to exploit its strong points and even enhance its limits. Very few other American bands can boast Aerosmith's power and capacity to pass from one genre to another without losing their basic nature. Indeed, when pop became their main 'style', they succeeded in improving their sound in a totally original way. An important part of American popular music, many other bands even look to them as an example of how to transform rock into present-day pop.

THE TYPICALLY FLAMBOYANT ON-STAGE BEHAVIOR OF STEVEN TYLER, VOCALIST AND FRONTMAN OF AEROSMITH, DURING A CONCERT IN DEL MAR, CALIFORNIA (2016).

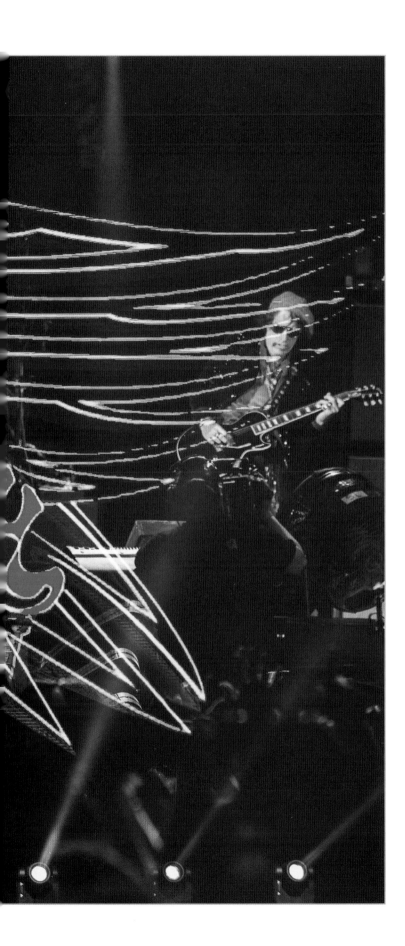

60-61 THE FAMOUS LOGO OF THE AMERICAN BAND AEROSMITH STANDS OUT ON STAGE DURING THEIR 2016 CONCERT IN SÃO PAULO, BRAZIL.

61 STEVEN TYLER, AT LEFT, AND JOE PERRY IN THEIR USUAL, UNORTHODOX APPAREL WHILE PERFORMING AT UNIONDALE, NEW YORK IN 2012.

Walk This Way

The song they've performed
live most often.

1970

The band is formed.

1972

Aerosmith signs a contract
with Columbia Records.

1975

Toys in the Attic is
released.

150

Number of records sold, in millions, around the world.

205

Number of songs, both originals and covers, Aerosmith has played live.

44

Times they have played the Beatles' *Helter Skelter*.

9

Number of musicians who have been members of the band.

8

Aerosmith songs that have been in the top ten in the United States.

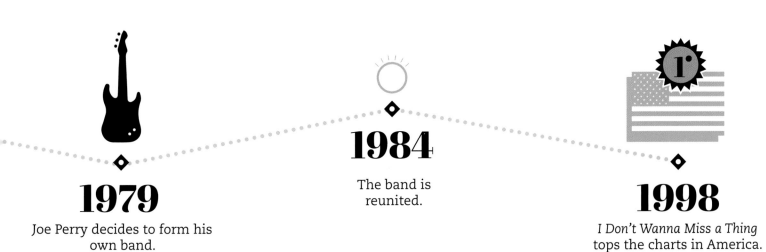

1979

Joe Perry decides to form his own band.

1984

The band is reunited.

1998

I Don't Wanna Miss a Thing tops the charts in America.

Bruce Springsteen

If rock has meaning, as it most surely does, it is precisely this: it is not just music and never has been just music; it is not a genre or a style, but something created magically from the fusion of a band on stage and an audience, an organism that lives and breathes, creates, walks, and produces art, passion and feeling. It also produces change, because each time you go to a rock concert, you leave a different person. And if not, if you are no different after a Bruce Springsteen concert, well, rock is not for you.

Springsteen and very few others today have this special power, the power to change people's lives through music. In his albums and concerts, Springsteen shows us that life is not necessarily what we imagine it to be, it may have unpleasant, devastating, absurd surprises in store for us. But at the same time, life can also be marvelous, overwhelming and unique. And whether you're rich or poor, sad or happy, there is always a new possibility, a promised land we must seek, a path to follow - together. Rhetoric? Perhaps, but frankly, who gives a damn? Springsteen's rhetoric and the dream of rock 'n' roll are for the better. Who wants to live a life without hope? Who is willing to forget about his dreams? Who doesn't want to imagine a better future? This is precisely what Springsteen offers during his concerts, what he communicates to his audience, giving them absolutely amazing evenings in exchange for their presence. He has sung this song since 1972, combining his stories and ours, the tale of a true, even legendary America that cinema, literature and music have helped build. Albums such as *Born to Run* and *Darkness on the Edge of Town* alone would be enough to categorize him among the greats, side by side with Bob Dylan and Paul Simon, Lennon & McCartney, Jagger & Richards, together with the great Beat poets and the millions of street poets who, with their guitars and voices, perform each evening in cafés and clubs on the outskirts of town, hoping for a moment of salvation - or perhaps offering salvation to those who listen to them. Springsteen and his E Street Band have performed for forty years now. They've had their ups and downs, but have never lost direct contact with the public, people, and life. And the more than 20 Grammy Awards won, the 120 million records sold, the 'sold out' tours in every corner of the planet do not matter that much. Success isn't what makes Bruce Springsteen great, but rather his credibility and faith. Because the Boss is a preacher, the high priest of the final rock ritual, the messiah of a community that is now split up and dispersed, a flock that he attempts to bring together again every evening. His effort and exertion are for the remission of our sins. His cry to the heavens is that of thousands of souls that refuse to give up. His rage and joy are the expression of hearts that, incredibly, beat in unison. Springsteen's songs are our songs, written by us, slices of life that become melodies, strophes and refrains running across our minds. In short, rock, only rock. Like the songs by the Beatles and Rolling Stones, the shout in *Won't Get Fooled Again*, Hendrix's guitar, *London Calling* by the Clash and *Seattle* by Nirvana. Rock, and nothing else.

64 BRUCE SPRINGSTEEN, THE STAR OF NEW JERSEY, PERFORMING WITH THE E STREET BAND AT THE OAKLAND COLISEUM IN CALIFORNIA IN 1984.

Bruce Springsteen

120

Number of records sold,
in millions.

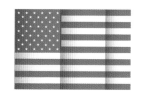

1,709

Estimated number of times that
Born to Run was performed live up
to the end of 2018.

310

The number of songs
Springsteen has 'officially'
composed. This is an
estimate, and the number
is much higher if we take
into account the many
bootlegs and songs sung by
other artists.

1976

Year in which Springsteen does
not release a single record, but
Taxi Driver, Martin Scorsese's
best-known film starring
Robert De Niro, comes out. The
famous monologue in front of
the mirror –"You talkin' to me?"
– refers to a joke by Springsteen
during one of his concerts
the year before, in which he
pretended not to understand
the audience's shouts of
enthusiasm.

1980

The year when one of
Springsteen's albums,
the double LP *The River*,
first topped the charts,
something that would
happen another ten times.

1999

Asteroid 23990 is renamed
Springsteen in his honor.

2000

Springsteen makes his
acting debut, playing
himself in an imaginary
dialog with the protagonist
of *High Fidelity*, John Cusack.

236

The performances of *Springsteen on Broadway* at the Walter Kerr Theater in New York, from 3 October 2017 to 15 December 2018.

246

The minutes (four hours and six minutes) of Springsteen's longest concert, held in Helsinki on 31 July 2012.

7

Singles from the bestseller *Born in the U.S.A.*, all of which were in the U.S. Top 10 in 1984-85.

31

Members of the band through the years, including wind instrumentalists and chorus members.

$ 18.95

Price of Springsteen's first guitar, which he bought in 1964, after watching the Beatles on the *Ed Sullivan Show*.

14

Months it took to record *Born to Run* (1974-75). The attention Springsteen paid to every detail became almost fanatical as regards the title track *Born to Run*, the recording of which lasted six months.

11

Members of the E Street Band from 1972 on. Three were replaced from 1974 to 1975, two died (Danny Federici in 2008, and Clarence Clemons in 2011), while six are still active (bassist Garry W. Tallent is the only member of the original lineup).

5

LPs in *Live 1975-85* (three discs in the CD version), a collection of tracks recorded at concerts released in 1986. It was the first and only box set of this size to top the charts.

2

Golden Globe awards received: one in 1994 for *Streets of Philadelphia* and one in 2009 for *The Wrestler*.

1

Number of Oscars won for *Streets of Philadelphia* in 1994.

It was precise day: 25 September 1976, a little more than 40 years ago. And a precise place: the kitchen of 14-year-old Larry Mullen Jr. in Dublin, Ireland. And a reason why seven youngsters attending the Mount Temple Comprehensive School should get together: to form a band. So it was an announcement on the school bulletin board that led to the birth of one of the greatest rock bands of all time, formed in the family kitchen of an adolescent drummer on the outskirts of town, where brothers David and Dick Evans, their friend Adam Clayton, two of Mullen's friends, Ivan McCormick and Peter Martin, and Paul Hewson met for the first time.

None of them thought they had a place in the world. But they were all searching for something and thought music might be a window that opened onto life. None of them really knew how to play an instrument. But their spirit was punk, a genre gaining steam at the time, leading them to pick up an instrument and go on stage. That afternoon was mostly spent conversing, getting to know one another, trying to understand if they shared the same dream. It seemed to work, so they set up another rehearsal, and then another and another. Thus they continued, with mangled cover songs, endless trials and poor instruments, month after month. They had even chosen a name: Feedback and then The Hype. But, like a plot twist in the best fables, something happened. Dick, Ivan and Peter went their own way, David became The Edge, Paul turned into Bono Vox, and the band became U2.

And U2 they are still today, with the same members, who have grown, changed, become rock stars, a legendary band playing rock music, that alchemical combination of rage, dreams, frenzy, passion and utopia that takes shape on stage and in records – alchemy that U2, like many other bands, is still able to transform into life. Their story is one of incredible friendship that still bonds them together, as well as a grand dream that led them to become the greatest rock band in the world from the late 1980s to the early 1990s. Their albums are a part of history, epic even; they've written songs that can still be heard every day on the radio around the world, in a style that has deeply influenced at least two generations of songwriters, guitarists and vocalists who came after them.

They have never been a 'lighthearted' band. Their social and political commitment, which is both personal and collective, has always fundamental; they have always taken sides, without hesitation, in battles they feel are important. This is especially true of Bono, who has even personally taken stands that challenge the powers that be. They have never been 'just' a rock band, but always something more, in keeping with their principles and mindset, keeping them active to this day, only the four of them, despite changing trends and fashions. They were avant-garde with Brian Eno and classical with Rattle & Hum; they have gone dance and electronic, melodic and sentimental. In short, they have been what every rock band worthy of the name must be – spectacular and surprising, bombastic and intimate. And they still are.

68 PORTRAITS OF U2. CLOCKWISE FROM ABOVE LEFT: THE EDGE, BONO, ADAM CLAYTON AND LARRY MULLEN JR.

70-71   U2 FRONTMAN BONO ON STAGE IN PARIS ON 18 JULY 2001, WHILE SHAKING HANDS WITH HIS FANS.

71   U2 GUITARIST THE EDGE, AND THE BAND'S VOCALIST BONO VOX ON STAGE AT THE MCI CENTER OF WASHINGTON. THEIR DEEP-FELT EMPATHY IS APPARENT IN EVERY CONCERT.

U2

1,009

The number of times U2 is estimated to have played *Pride (In the Name of Love)* live, the song most performed in full. *Sunday Bloody Sunday* has been played 928 times; however, if we add the famous self-referential snippets, this song has been played 1029 times, putting it in first place.

500

The number, in millions, of those who in 2014 listened to the newly-released *Songs of Innocence* on iTunes, an album made available without charge thanks to an investment by Apple reported to have amounted to $100 million.

12

Runtime, in minutes, of the version of *Bad* played at Live Aid on 13 July 1985. During the performance, broadcast on TV sets around the world, Bono walked out into the audience and embraced a girl, protecting her from the crowd.

6

Number of people who replied to the notice placed by Larry Mullen Jr. on the bulletin board of Mount Temple Comprehensive School in Dublin in 1976. Three of them formed U2 with him. For a short time, it was called The Larry Mullen Band, until Paul 'Bono' Hewson arrived.

5

Songs released as singles taken from *Achtung Baby*, the album marking U2's total re-invention of its sound and image (1991-92).

1976

The band is formed in Dublin.

1980

The first U2 album is released.

1987

U2 achieves international fame. Over 5 million copies of *The Joshua Tree* have been sold, making U2 the most important band in the 1980s (even appearing on the cover of *Time* Magazine), as well as the most popular band in the last 30 years.

1991

Achtung Baby is released, the band's turning point.

30

Height, in meters (98 feet), of the huge yellow arch, an explicit reference to the McDonald's logo, which stood in the middle of the gigantic stage of the U2's 1997 PopMart Tour. The largest audience on the tour was the one in Reggio Emilia, Italy, with more than 150,000 paying spectators.

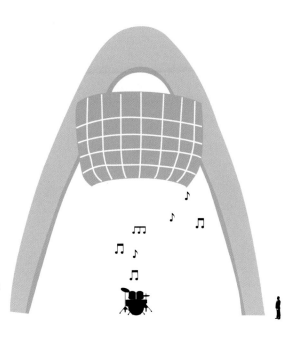

24

The record number of snippets and fragments of more or less classical songs that Bono habitually inserts in live performances. On November 28, 2015 in Dublin, he played 24 snippets in 26 songs.

3 ♪♪♪

Number of songs on the first EP, aptly titled *Three* and released in 1979, a year before their debut LP, *Boy*.

2

The maximum number of albums Steve Lillywhite had previously produced with a single artist or band. He finally went for a third with U2's *War*, which turned out to be the band's first no. 1 album on the English charts.

2005

U2 is inducted into the Rock and Roll Hall of Fame by Bruce Springsteen (the first year they were eligible).

2009

The year of the 360° Tour, their highest grossing tour of all.

2017

Songs of Experience is released, for free, on iTunes.

Dire Straits

If you search the internet for one of the many 'best rock guitarist' lists drawn up by fans, you will often find the name Mark Knopfler near the top. This is, quite simply, because he deserves to be considered one of the world's six-string masters, especially since Knopfler arrived on the scene at a unique moment, shortly after the explosion of punk and just in time for the arrival of a 'new wave' that had repudiated 'old-fashioned' guitars, opting for electronic keyboards. And for those who insisted on using the good old six strings, it was best if they didn't have a particularly good technique and reject all forms of virtuosity and related solos. But Knopfler, an outlier, based his success precisely on the latter. With Dire Straits, he managed to retain the spirit of new wave, creating music that was totally against the tide, but based on guitar playing, Knopfler's solos, and virtuosity. To be more precise, he was 'timeless', and has always been so. Yet he has never abandoned his close contact with contemporary life (for example, *Money for Nothing* and its not-so-subtle criticism of the MTV generation), a space in which Dire Straits felt totally at ease, thus allowing those who could not grasp new wave or punk to continue to enjoy rock without being labeled as old fogies. This sentimental, passionate band became legendary, selling more than 120 million albums, but

when their projects began to lose their intensity, Knopfler thought it was time to pack his bags and go elsewhere. The Scottish guitarist's 'elsewhere' proved to be a spectacular and boundless landscape of sound. It would be unfair to claim his decision was based entirely on nostalgia, which indeed is part and parcel of his expression, with his many references to blues, country, Celtic music and folk music in general. No, Knopfler knew how to look beyond; he knew how to interpret tradition in a highly personal manner and, as in the Dire Straits period, without ever losing sight of the current scene. Knopfler is in step with the times, but in his very own way, as he has always been, moving intelligently in many different directions, creating fantastic settings that traverse epochs and sounds. In short, he moves freely in a vast sea of music. And his guitar-playing style, the magnificent fingerpicking for which he is famous, has improved with time and become even more refined and sensual, while remaining measured and essential. Never uselessly spectacular, never unrestrained or vain, Knopfler shows us that he loves the guitar and its sound perhaps to a greater degree than his more-famous peers. Knopfler continues to offer us the sound of his guitar and that of Dire Straits, a band that still takes us on a fantasy trip into its highly personal, romantic world.

74   THE MEMBERS OF DIRE STRAITS IN 1978. CLOCKWISE FROM LEFT: JOHN ILLSLEY, DAVID KNOPFLER, PICK WHITERS AND MARK KNOPFLER.

Dire Straits

400,000

Copies of the single
Sultans of Swing sold in
the United Kingdom in 1978;
yet it was only 8th on the charts.

248

The number of 'sold out' Dire
Straits concerts in 1985 and 1986,
including the historic Live Aid
concert.

LIVE AID

24

The sidemen who have
collaborated in the recordings of
the band during its long career.

1977

The formation of Dire
Straits, a rock quartet
in the middle of a punk
tempest.

1983

Bob Dylan selects Mark
Knopfler as the producer of
his album *Infidels*.

120

Records the band has sold, in millions, all over the world.

14

The runtime, in minutes (plus a few more seconds), of *Telegraph Road*, the band's longest and most ambitious piece.

 # 9

The film soundtracks recorded by the guitar virtuoso.

7

Grammy Awards won by Knopfler, both with Dire Straits and as a solo artist.

6

The band's studio albums, plus three live ones and three compilations.

1989

Knopfler creates the soundtrack of *Last Exit to Brooklyn* and then forms the informal alternative country band The Notting Hillbillies, with Steve Phillips, Brendan Croker and, later, Guy Fletcher.

1995

Dire Straits disbands in order to allow Knopfler to concentrate on his career as a soloist.

Oasis

Any hypothetical rating of the greatest English rock bands of the last thirty years would have to place the Oasis near the top of the list. Whether you like them or not, you must admit that Oasis is one of the bands that truly represented British rock in the 1990s. In fact, Oasis is 'Brit' in the most credible and interesting sense, having alternated periods of great creativity and success with others that were decidedly less so. After the explosion of punk and new wave, after the rise of electronica, what did rock have to contribute? Oasis tried to answer this difficult question by producing 'Brit rock' that was elegant and refined, yet could still manage to 'keep up with the times'. And that's exactly what Oasis did, achieving sensational and well-deserved success as a result of the band's exceptional creativity and effortless compositions, somewhere between pop and rock but more complex, rich and profound than much of the music played by their contemporaries. The creativity and style of Liam and Noel Gallagher's band was such that it was often likened to the Beatles. Obviously this comparison is difficult, if not downright impossible, to make: the periods, youth culture, and world in which their musical styles grew and developed are too different. Yet it has some truth to it, because Oasis departed from the Beatles in order to lend new meaning to English rock and pop; modeled on Lennon & McCartney to try, once again, to embody the world and youth culture at

an important, singular time, when the Gallagher's hometown of Manchester was becoming the center of the world. And it was precisely for this reason that, unlike the bands belonging to other British musical trends, Oasis and a few others (such as Blur) did not rapidly fall out of fashion. To the contrary, they belonged to a generation that, after years of American domination, succeeded in regaining their musical foothold, influencing the behavior and fashions of teens and twenty-somethings everywhere while trying to make the music less about sales and more about substance. Without a doubt, the Oasis hairdo, as well as style, which was closely connected to mod fashion, lent a 'British' touch to the entire project. Yet this was not empty, superficial costuming. They were simple, explicit choices that fans could identify with, and the millions of copies of albums sold abundantly attest to this. Great albums, many concerts and memorable songs have made Oasis one of the leading turn-of-the-millennium British bands, central to the development of rock that came after them – despite the fact that the Gallagher brothers' constant fights culminated in the break-up of the band, preventing it from achieving even more. But Oasis' style, indisputable elegance, and ability to revive elements of the past and transform them into the music of today, are still current and beloved by music fans, who have not forgotten the Gallagher brothers one bit.

78   OASIS, FROM MANCHESTER, PHOTOGRAPHED ON A LONDON STREET IN 1994. FROM LEFT: PAUL MCGUIGAN, NOEL GALLAGHER, LIAM GALLAGHER, PAUL 'BONEHEAD' ARTHURS AND TONY MCCARROLL.

Oasis

1992

Oasis plays its first concert.

1998

The band wins first prize at the *Brit Awards* with their album *Be Here Now*.

2009

Oasis breaks up for good after the umpteenth furious argument between the Gallagher brothers.

22

Number, in millions, of copies sold of (*What's the Story*) *Morning Glory?* Besides being the band's most famous album, it was also among the best-selling records of all time in the United Kingdom, ranked among Queen's *Greatest Hits* and the Beatles' *Sgt. Pepper*.

40,000

Tickets sold, in just three hours, for the first night at Maine Road in Manchester, UK as part of the promotional tour for (*What's the Story*) *Morning Glory?* held at.

10,000

The number of Dutch carnations used to shoot the video for *Don't Look Back in Anger* (3,000 were artificially colored blue).

589

Number of times Oasis has performed the song *Cigarettes and Alcohol* live.

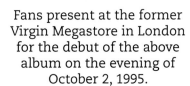 **300**

Fans present at the former Virgin Megastore in London for the debut of the above album on the evening of October 2, 1995.

 **10**

Various members and sidemen that played in the band over the years.

2:

The only stable members of the band for its entire existence, Liam and Noel Gallagher.

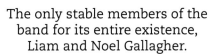

Blues

The blues is more than 100 years old and, frankly, it doesn't look it. It's history is so rich, so topical, that every new generation considers it modern, its 'own'. Decade after decade, the blues is reborn, starting from scratch again and again. It doesn't matter if the songs resemble each another, if the performances of a modern-day bluesman and one who lived 100 years ago don't differ much. There may be only one kind blues or 100,000, but by now the blues is part of us, hidden in the groove of every song, preserved in the depths of the heart, ready to describe a lost love, a dream, a hope, or a simple, normal day, ready to become a secret, private diary once again or the context for a multi-voiced popular tale.

Blues music is everywhere around us. It's in pop, which has taken the blues' life-blood of stories of love and desperation to narrate the truth. It's in rock music, which, without those three chords, would probably never have been born. Blues is in rap and hip hop, the root that anchors the tree of new African American music, allowing it to grow. There is blues in jazz,

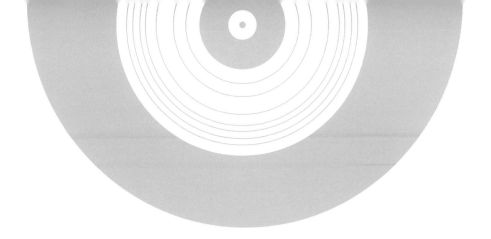

folk, classical and opera, in soul and R&B, and even in house music, because the blues is everywhere. It is in the blood that flows in the veins of any musician, even those who think they have never played blues in their life.

Obviously, the blues is a style and a sound; it has its own structure and rules. But what counts in order to be a true bluesman is to 'have the blues', which is much more than simply knowing how to play or sing it. The blues is therefore a condition of the spirit, in which melancholy and joy, desperation and hope manage to coexist, just as it was for African Americans at the beginning of the 20th century. Picking up guitars to create a brand new genre of music, African American communities put their new social status to music: no longer slaves but always last in line.

Blues music had a magnificent myriad of heroes, but the list of important blues musicians is much too long to quote here. Its guitarists, pianists and singers traveled all over the world with songs that have become the foundation of an incredibly huge, majestic and glorious musical temple – the great house of blues, the doors of which are always open, ready to welcome anyone who has a fine story to tell.

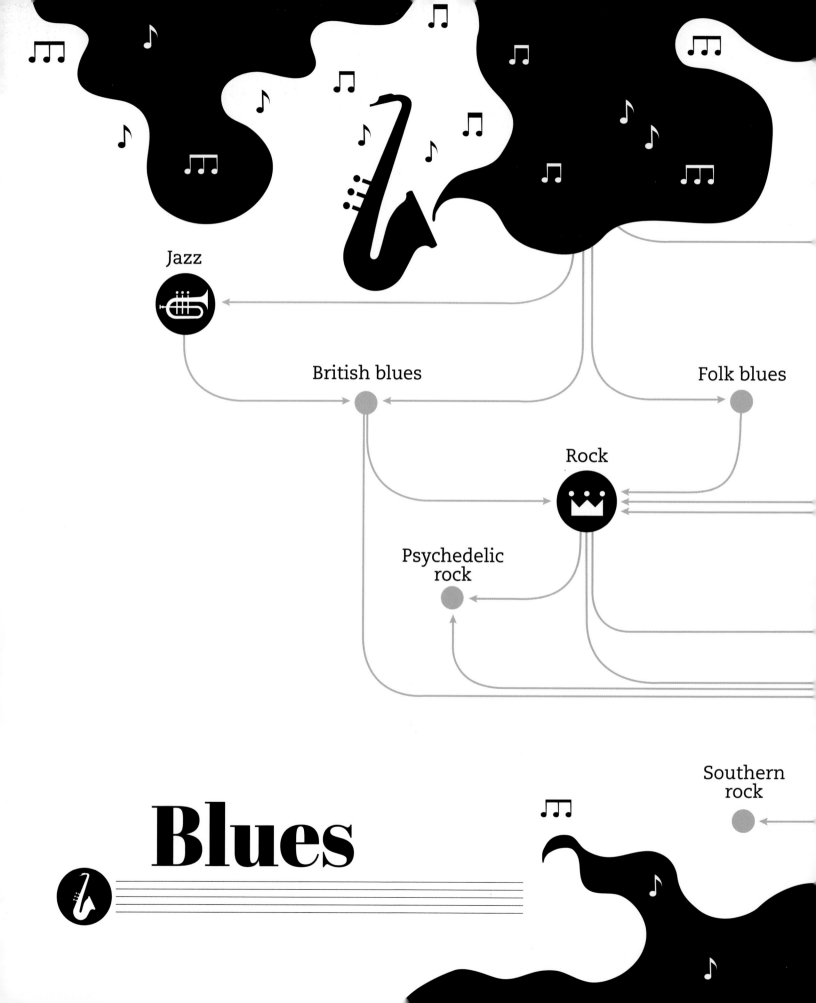

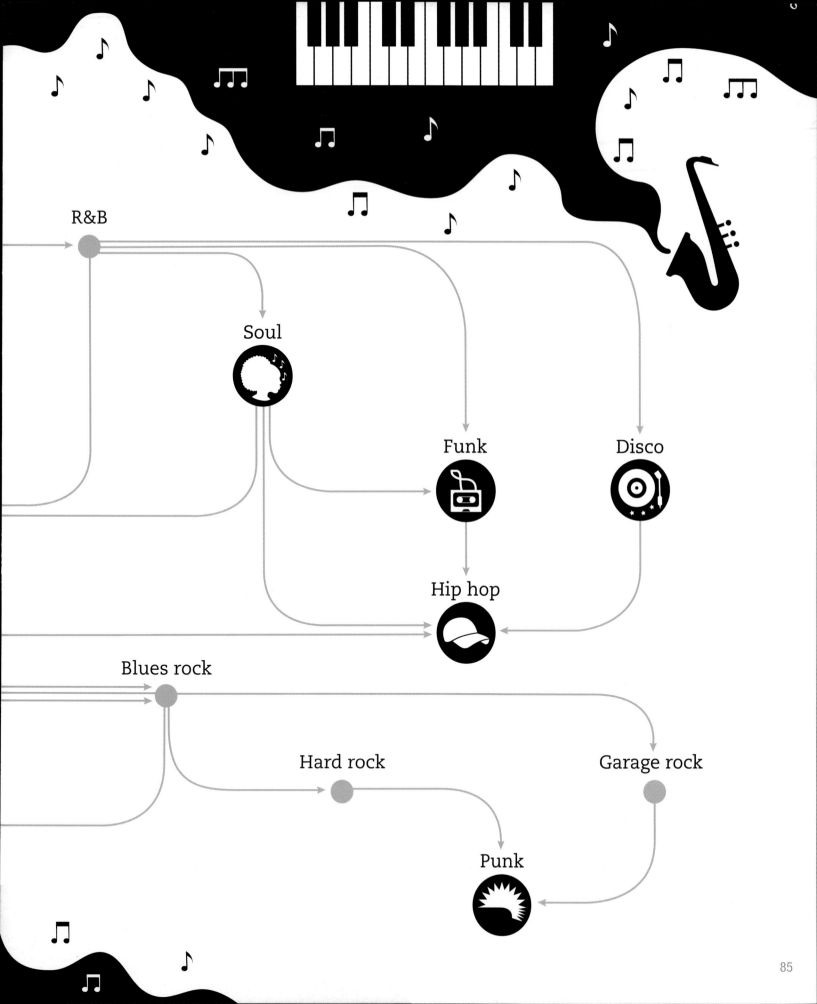

R&B

Soul

Funk

Disco

Hip hop

Blues rock

Hard rock

Garage rock

Punk

The Rolling Stones

When someone mentions the Rolling Stones, you immediately know what they're talking about. An entire universe opens up before your eyes and, most importantly, your ears. The band's fundamental albums – *Sticky Fingers, Beggar's Banquet, Let It Bleed, Exile on Main Street, Some Girls* and all the others – are precious gemstones that form an essential part of any personal record collection, since the Stones' story belongs not just to the band, but to us as well.

Sex, drugs and rock 'n' roll? Sure, but, let's not limit ourselves to the obvious, the usual 'pact with the devil', the infinite number of anecdotes concerning Keith Richards and his drug addiction, the 'eternal youth' (despite the many deep wrinkles) of the members of the band, each of whom has in some way survived all kinds of problems and outrageous behavior. No, the Stones are so much more than that.

A little more than 50 years ago, in 1965, they sparked a rock explosion with a single song, *Satisfaction*. By itself, it would have been enough to earn them a place in the history of modern popular music and Western culture. That track, simple, direct and mechanically infallible because it is based on a riff that with a circular movement penetrates your memory for good, embodied something known to every young person on the planet: the world, as it was, offered no satisfaction. Through power and simplicity, taking the blues and transforming it into rock, the Rolling Stones lit a new fuse of youthful rebellion.

It is all too easy to relegate the Stones to their 'folklore'. In fact, it seems as if they've done everything they can to confirm the clichés about the 'beautiful and damned', the princes of excess and transgression. So, putting them in that box once again would only be a disservice.

The band is one of the cornerstones (which do not roll) of modern popular culture and contemporary music. Together with the Beatles, Dylan, the Who, Pink Floyd, David Bowie and a few others, the Rolling Stones have made an essential contribution to the world we now live in, our freedom of expression, our lifestyle and culture, cinema, literature, and television. If it's necessary to read the classics of literature, it's also necessary to listen to the classics of rock. Those who have never listened to and admired the music of the Rolling Stones have missed an important part of 20th-century music; they are simply unaware of things they should be familiar with. Those who have listened to and loved Mick & Co., on the other hand, often think differently about music and the way they listen to it.

86   THE ROLLING STONES POSING FOR PHOTOGRAPHERS IN THE 1960S. FROM LEFT: MICK JAGGER, KEITH RICHARDS, BILL WYMAN, BRIAN JONES AND, BELOW, CHARLIE WATTS.

But most importantly, they have added something to their cultural experience; they have discovered new thrills, emotions and excitement. After all, the five (now four) Rolling Stones have never been a band offering only entertainment. They weren't at the beginning, when as zealous devotees of jazz and blues they tried to teach younger generations about the roots of American music, the essence of modern sound, the expressive potential of a few chords or a simple riff - enough to recount an entire life. And they weren't in the following years when, up to the mid-1970s, they wrote, played and created some of the most important albums in the history of rock. And they aren't today, when their extraordinary circus demonstrates that their music is anything but dead and gone. Without exaggeration, we could say that the world without the Rolling Stones would not be the same; it would be worse. If you listen to them today, your life may still change. Give it a try.

88-89 THE ROLLING STONES ON STAGE AT THE VELODROME IN MAR-SEILLES ON JUNE 26, 2018 DURING THEIR NO FILTER TOUR.

The Rolling Stones

120

Singles released by the Rolling Stones.

750

The approximate amount, in millions of dollars, the band grossed during their tours.

7

The millions of dollars the band received for a private concert given for a Texas millionaire.

8

Songs that were no. 1 hits on the British charts.

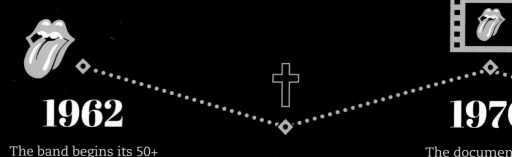

1962

The band begins its 50+ year career, which is still in progress.

1969

The year of the death of Brian Jones, the founder of the band.

1970

The documentary on the Rolling Stones, *Gimme Shelter*, is released (directed by Albert and David Maysles). One of the camera operators is a 25-year-old George Lucas.

1971

Sticky Fingers is released with an actual zipper on the cover designed by Andy Warhol.

10

Songs that were censored, banned by the BBC or by Chinese authorities during the band's Asian tours, or strongly contested due to their 'controversial' content – despite their great popularity and ranking on the charts.

81

Albums in the Stones discography: 30 studio recordings, 26 live, and 25 compilations.

45

Tours that took the quintet to every corner of the earth.

22

Musicians who collaborated with the Stones either in the studio or on tour without ever being considered official members of the band.

10

Movies in which superstar Mick Jagger has acted. He was also a candidate for the role of Alex in Kubrick's *A Clockwork Orange,* and in Jodorowsky's *Dune,* which was never finished.

9

Number of Mick Jagger's children. He also has five grandchildren and one great grandchild, Ezra Key, the daughter of his grandchild Assisi.

5

Permanent members of the band, with only three replacements: Mick Taylor and then Ron Wood, who replaced the late Brian Jones, and Darryl Jones, who replaced Bill Wyman as bassist in 1994 (without ever becoming an official member).

The ranking of *(I Can't Get No) Satisfaction* on the 500 Greatest Songs of all Time according to *Rolling Stone.*

1

Number of songs written by Lennon & McCartney that the Rolling Stones made a great success: *I Wanna Be Your Man.*

1972

The band goes into 'tax exile' in the Côte d'Azur, where they record their album *Exile on Main Street.*

1985

Ian Stewart, Rolling Stones' drummer, dies.

1989

The band is inducted to the Rock and Roll Hall of Fame.

2016

The Stones is the first band to play a concert in Cuba after sanctions are lifted.

Eric Clapton

Eric Clapton was born on March 30, 1945 in Ripley, Surrey County, England. His nickname is 'Slowhand', presumably because his guitar strings would often break when he was on stage, and while he was replacing them the audience would give him a slow clap or 'slow hand'. Clapton has been concertizing for 50 years, playing both with bands that have helped to write blues rock history and as a world famous soloist who has adopted different musical styles over the years, from traditional blues to psychedelic rock, reggae and pop rock, still going strong today. He belongs to the extraordinary generation of English guitarists born in the mid-1940s that paved the way for modern rock and literally invented the modern-day 'guitar hero'. Clapton is arguably the only one in this group who can also be considered a concert artist par excellence in all categories. Everything considered, he's an individual who cannot bear band life and whose musical experience has been decisive for the evolution of rock. His career is studded with short-lived but major events: his sensational debut with the John Mayall and the Bluesbreakers (Mayall was an incredible mentor to just about every famous blues and blues rock musician known today); his stint with the Yardbirds; the glorious yet tempestuous collaboration with Cream, together with Jack Bruce and Ginger Baker; his period with one of the first super bands in history, Blind Faith; and then with Delaney & Bonnie and Derek and the Dominos (where he met Duane Allman).

So it is quite natural that, as legend has it, he refused an offer to join the Beatles when Harrison left the band. Clapton was too close a friend to Harrison (who in the meantime had returned to the band) and, as he himself said in one of the splendid *Beatles Anthology* DVDs, he wasn't made for playing in a band. Despite this, a short time later he agreed to play on the first album recorded by John Lennon and Yoko Ono's Plastic Ono Band. Like many of his colleagues, he too has suffered existential problems and struggles: the discovery that he was raised by his grandparents and not his parents; that the person he believed to be his sister was really his mother; the fact that he never knew his father; addiction to drugs and alcohol that virtually stole him away from music; and his remorse at having fallen in love with George Harrison's wife (which inspired one of his masterpieces, *Layla*). He emerged triumphant from all this and has continued along the path to glory up to the present, even in spite of the tragic, absurd death of his son Conor, who fell out of the window of a New York City skyscraper. That terrible experience led Clapton to write *Tears In Heaven*, one of the most famous songs in his repertoire. In the meantime, in Antigua, he founded a rehab clinic called Crossroads, sharing a name with the masterpiece by Robert Johnson and the festival Clapton organizes every year, inviting the best guitarists in the world. Though he continues tirelessly in the recording studio, Clapton hasn't played live for some time, even if every once in a while he appears on stage with a friend, especially with Steve Winwood, with whom he has shared most of his long career. Like Jimi Hendrix, Jimmy Page and few others, Clapton is the very essence of a rock guitarist – a title he will hold for quite a long time.

92 ERIC CLAPTON, NICKNAMED 'SLOWHAND' FOR HIS UNIQUE STYLE, DURING A CONCERT AT THE AHOY ROTTERDAM ARENA ON APRIL 23, 1983.

93

Eric Clapton

$ 850,000

The amount, in dollars, paid at an auction for Eric Clapton's modified black Fender Stratocaster, which he called Blackie.

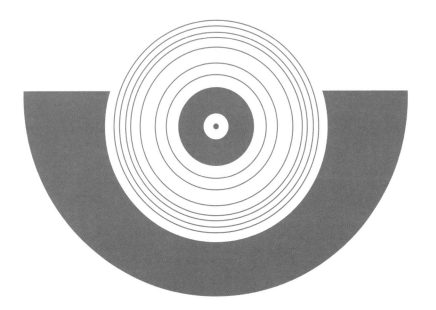

100

Copies of albums sold, in millions, worldwide.

37

Collaborations on albums by other musicians.

1945

Eric Patrick Clapton is born in Ripley, Surrey County, England.

1965

The year Clapton debuts with the Yardbirds.

1966

Cream is formed.

1974

461 *Ocean's Boulevard*, Clapton's first true solo album, is released.

13

Albums on which Clapton is credited together with the Beatles (*White Album*), and with soloists George Harrison and Ringo Starr.

3

Times Clapton was inducted to the Rock and Roll Hall of Fame: as a soloist and as a member of the Yardbirds and Cream.

8

Number of bands he has played in.

2

Position on *Rolling Stone*'s 100 Greatest Guitarists of All Time.

1992

Clapton writes *Tears in Heaven*, dedicated to his four year-old son Conor, who died in an accident.

2004

Clapton becomes a Commander of the Order of the British Empire.

2007

His autobiography is published.

2017

The year of his official return on the stage.

Janis. That's what she's been called for quite a while, from the time of her untimely death at 27, at the peak of her career, in the full bloom of youth, and in the midst of her personal tragedy. Just Janis, because her voice penetrates the soul, her music is bonded with our hearts. The art and life of Janis Joplin are one and the same, an inextricable tangle in which it is impossible to separate reality from representation, music in which the voice truly mirrors the soul, without dissimulation. Joplin was born and raised in Texas, but she was in her element in San Francisco, in the phenomenal psychedelic cauldron that was boiling at Haight & Ashbury, at the Fillmore Auditorium and the Avalon Ballroom, at the early festivals and free concerts in the streets and squares, among the hippies and revolutionaries who dreamed of changing the world. It was here that Janis set out to redefine the blues, mixing it with the colors and emotions of a generation focused on desires and dreams. Hers was a world where everything seemed to consist of peace, love and music. And love was precisely what was lacking for the incredibly talented woman who learned the blues by listening to the great African American singers of the past, shaping old sounds into a contemporary form, rock, the perfect way to convey new ideas and images. The rise of blues rock in the mid-1960s in California clearly bears her name, because Joplin had succeeded in passionately and rebelliously interpreting the 'blues revival' without betraying its spirit or questioning its fundamental canons. To Joplin, the blues was alive and well, there was no need to revive it. Instead, to the old magic of blues, she brought a contemporary heart and soul that was different from the others roaming the streets of hippie California, imagining the world they wanted to live in. Three albums in all, from 1967 to 1969 – two of which were recorded with Big Brother and the Holding Company, and one as a soloist – marked the beginning of an adventure that never materialized, because Joplin died on October 4, 1970 of a heroin overdose. A terrible death, especially considering the album she was working on, *Pearl,* released posthumously: the finest in her career, the one that not only expressed her passion and desperation, but also life, hope and the vision of a tomorrow that never arrived. Joplin was one of the greatest singers of all, one of the very few voices in white America able to interpret blues with the right spirit, to inject it with soul, to sing according to the volatile nature of human emotions.

Janis Joplin

19

Number of compilations, all posthumous.

8

Number of posthumous live albums.

4

Albums in her discography recorded live (two with Big Brother, two as a soloist).

1943

Janis Lyn Joplin is born in Port Arthur, Texas.

1964

Joplin and the future guitarist of Jefferson Airplane, Jorma Kaukonen, record their first blues standards.

1965

Joplin forms her first band, Big Brother and the Holding Company.

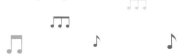

1967

A triumph at the Monterey Pop Festival.

1968

Cheap Thrills, one of the most important albums with San Francisco's psychedelic sound, tops the *Billboard* charts. It is now ranked no. 338 on *Rolling Stone's* 500 Greatest Albums of All Time.

1969

Joplin sings in the era-defining three-day Woodstock Festival with her new group, the Kozmic Blues Band.

98 JANIS JOPLIN AT WOODSTOCK IN AUGUST 1969. SHE INTERPRETED THE BLUES WITH OVER-POWERING EMOTION.

99 A 1970 PORTRAIT OF THE GREAT BLUES AND ROCK SINGER FROM TEXAS, JANIS JOPLIN.

Jimi Hendrix

There was a time when Jimi was Jimmy, a boy from Seattle born on November 27, 1942. There was a time when young Jimmy suffered due to his parents' separation, the death of his mother and the challenges his brothers and sisters faced – a time when he found consolation in music. There was a time when Jimi was still Jimmy and made a living playing his guitar in American nightclubs as a backing musician along with his friend and fellow guitarist Billy Cox, whom Jimmy met when he enlisted in the army at the age of 17, and with whom he had formed a club band. There was even a time when Jimmy was a sideman for dozens of both unknown and famous musicians, including the Isley Brothers and King Curtis. But Jimmy wanted to become Jimi, and he wanted to play his guitar his very own way. After all, his guitar was his most faithful friend, which, like a crystal ball, revealed the future to him, a ship upon which he journeyed into the sea of music in search of unknown lands. For Hendrix, working for others was limiting. He wanted to do something else, to prove to the world that his music and vision of the blues were different. He had discovered Dylan and English rock, and now had to begin to soar.

The opportunity to become Jimi was offered to him by Chas Chandler, the star of the Animals, who had heard him play in America (according to legend, *Hey Joe* was the song that convinced Chandler of Hendrix's talent) and took him to England, where he recorded his first single (*Hey Joe*, of course*)*. Released in 1966, it put the Jimi Hendrix Experience (which also included drummer Mitch Mitchell and bassist Noel Redding) at the center of the music scene. London became his second home, the place where he could finally 'let loose' and vent all his creative talent. He stayed there for 18 months before going back to the United States, like a king returning from exile, ready to hold the scepter once again and also bask in his personal triumph. The following two years were full of ups and downs, a rush of concerts and recording sessions, drugs, alcohol and women – all in massive doses.

And then there was his guitar, a means and an end, an instrument and a cult, an object of desire and the map upon which Hendrix constantly searched for his island. No one before, and no one after Hendrix had used or would use the guitar in the same way. His unparalleled, inimitable style combined captivating spectacle and invention; it married technique and innovation. Every note in his solos seemed to be there for a specific reason, part of an ineluctable destiny – not only fascination and mystery, but also the expression of an inner reality that amazingly came to light.

Then came the end, his tragic death at the age of twenty-seven, followed by his legend, legacy and the numerous posthumous albums that have helped us to discover previously-unknown, beautiful musical moments. But above all, they also help us understand his need for music and his torrential creativity, with all the ups and downs they entailed. Hendrix was without a doubt the most important and innovative electric guitarist of the 20th century, and in many respects his music is still contemporary and powerful.

100   JIMI HENDRIX IN A PHOTOGRAPH FROM THE COVER OF *ELECTRIC LADYLAND* (1968).

Jimi Hendrix

340,000

The asking auction price, in pounds, for the Fender Stratocaster that Hendrix is believed to have burned at the London Astoria in 1967 or Miami Pop in 1968. Frank Zappa was given the guitar, then restored and played it. Zappa's son held an auction for it in 2002, but no buyers came forth who were willing to pay the starting bid price.

32,000

The amount, in dollars, Hendrix received for his appearance at Woodstock.

35

Amount, in U.S. cents, Hendrix earned for his first concert with the Rocking Kings.

1964

Hendrix records *Testify* with the Isley Brothers.

1942

James Marshall Hendrix is born in Seattle on November 27.

1961

Hendrix is a parachutist in the 101st Airborne Division.

1966

On December 16, *Hey Joe* 45 is released in Europe. It is the first Jimi Hendrix Experience single (a cover whose composition is attributed to Billy Roberts), and the song that would close out the Woodstock Festival.

19

The women who appear on the cover of *Electric Ladyland*.

9

The number of Vesparax sleeping pills he took the night he died.

1,881

Guitarists who played *Hey Joe* simultaneously in the main square of Wroclaw, Poland in 2007 (setting a Guinness world record and breaking the previous record set a year earlier in the same town, with 'only' 1,572 guitarists).

684

Titles in Hendrix's overall discography according to the Discogs site.

600

Number of concerts Hendrix played from 1966 to 1970.

282

Number of weeks Hendrix's albums were in the Top 75.

27

Hendrix's age when he died in London in September 1970. He would have turned 28 a little more than two months later.

23

Days between the formation of the Experience band and its first album.

1967

The Jimi Hendrix Experience goes on a short tour in England, playing with Keith Emerson's the Nice, with the Move and Eire Apparent, and with Syd Barrett's Pink Floyd. The debut album *Are You Experienced?* is released the same year.

1968

The year his Electric Lady Studio is inaugurated in New York.

1970

The year of his death in London.

0

The times he topped the charts. *Are you Experienced?* had the best ranking, arriving at no. 2.

7

The years of Hendrix's musical career.

4

Number of Hendrix albums released when he was alive.

/Pop

When we talk about pop music, what are we really talking about? Apparently it's something light, music written to be sung in the shower, danced to in a club, or heard quickly in a video clip and then forgotten in a couple of months. Yet, this seemingly 'superfluous' genre has become part and parcel of everyday life, including that of people who are not familiar with it, or openly declare they do not like it. Yet all music has a soul and, whether we like it or not, pop is the soul of today.

Yes, pop is the soul of those who live their everyday lives with passion and pain, happiness and hopelessness, problems both big and little, dreams and drama. Pop speaks to us about life as it is and also how we would like it to be. Pop is the common language of a certain segment of the global population, the one that thinks freedom is the high road to conquer the world. It's over the top, colorful, brazen, sexy, extravagant; it's sentimental, obvious, magnificently banal, and it packs everything neatly into to basic feelings and key words; it doesn't require introspection yet it seeks truth. Pop is stupid, and so are we, more than we'd like to admit. Pop is overwhelming; it sets our

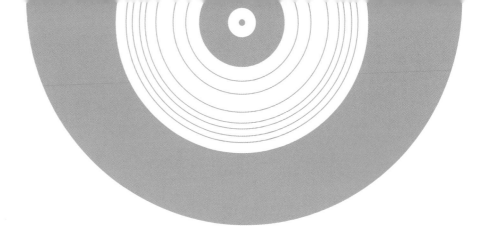

hearts aflame. It's simple, made up of the simplicity at the heart of our desires. It is always fresh, even though it's always the same. It's music that says "I love you," "I miss you," "you're beautiful," "let's stay together" and a host of other phrases and words that are ours. Pop is what we want to be but cannot be. It animates our days because by presenting its own reality, it makes life seem better. Pop makes us weep and laugh, it puts us in a good mood and is beside us during moments of melancholy; it makes us dance and gets our bodies in sync with the rhythm of life. Pop doesn't ask us to change the world, but rather to experience it; it doesn't help us discover things we don't know, instead, it knows us. Pop may seem commercial and vacuous, shallow and light-hearted, useless and perhaps, in some cases, even damaging and ignorant. But upon a closer look, its shallow splendor is what conceals all its magnificence, its total and absolute freedom, its amazing vital force and perfect joy. Moreover, among the entertainers, showgirls, boy bands and pop stars, there are also great artists, songwriters penning unforgettable masterpieces, singers who can make us cry or laugh with a couple of notes, performers who present not only their shows, but our existence as well. They are those who, between one refrain and another, declare their allegiance to freedom, excess, sex, joy, love, community, creativity, entertainment, and life.

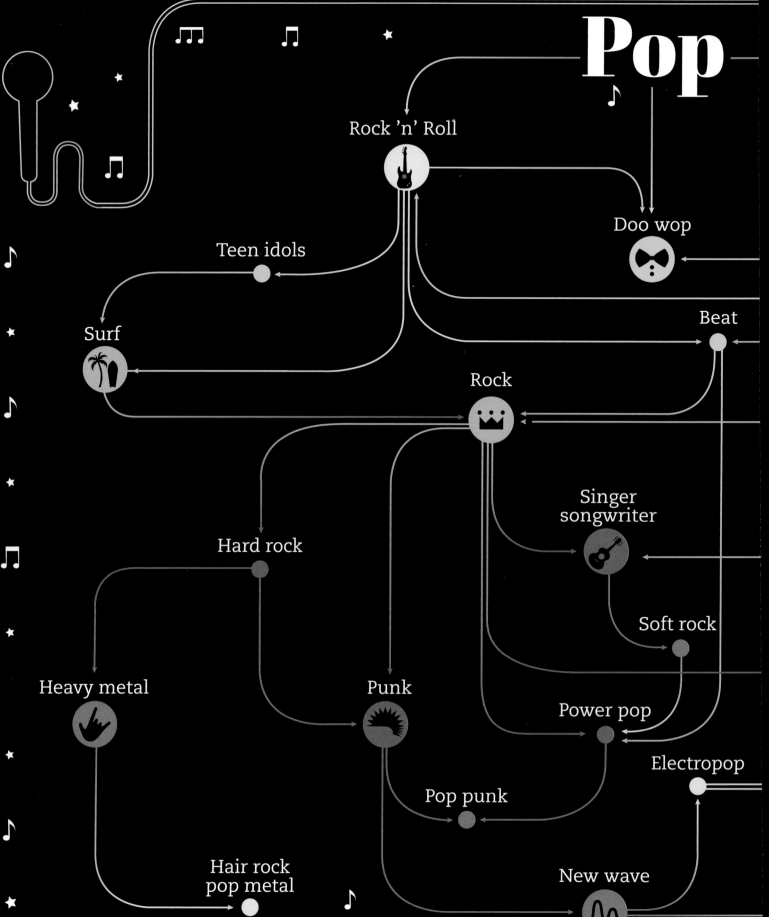

Pop

Rock 'n' Roll

Doo wop

Teen idols

Beat

Surf

Rock

Singer
songwriter

Hard rock

Soft rock

Heavy metal

Punk

Power pop

Electropop

Pop punk

Hair rock
pop metal

New wave

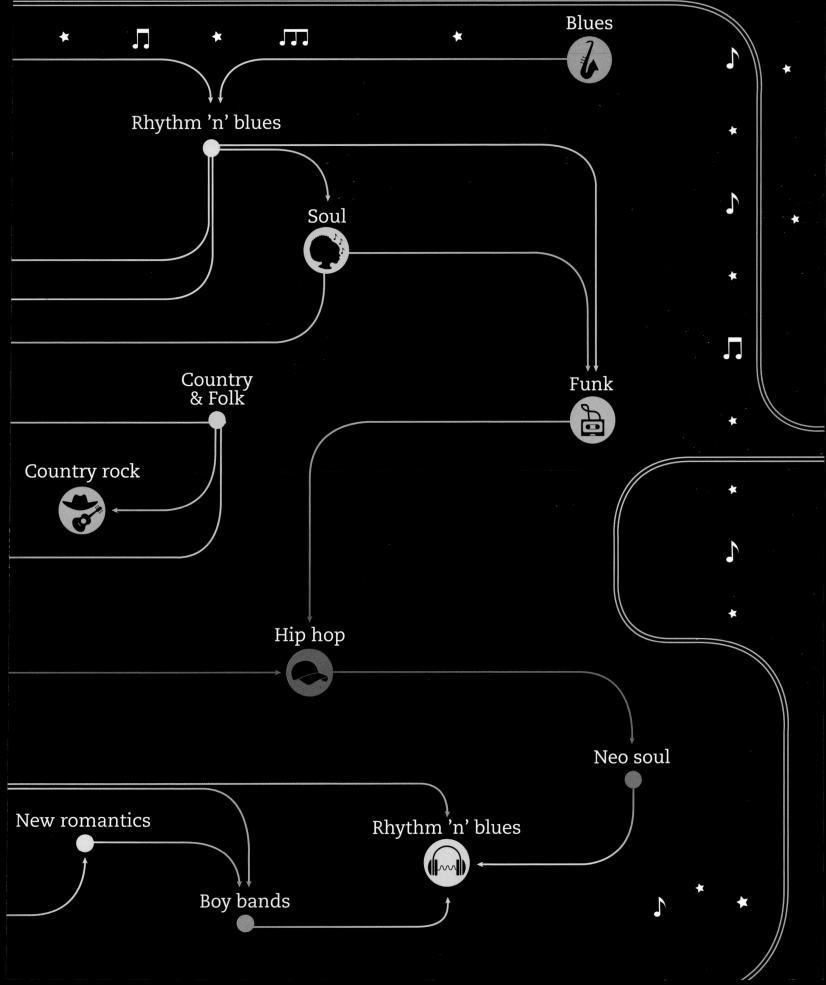

Blues

Rhythm 'n' blues

Soul

Country & Folk

Country rock

Funk

Hip hop

Neo soul

New romantics

Rhythm 'n' blues

Boy bands

David Bowie

Rock simply wouldn't be the same without him. David Bowie was not only one of the greatest artists that rock produced, but also a thinker, an innovator, an icon, a model, a source of inspiration, a central figure for 50 years of pop culture. Bowie was an extraordinarily creative musician with an androgynous, mysterious look, a fantastic and surprising mime, actor, rock star and experimenter. From the 1970s to the early 2000s, his presence and works deeply influenced the collective imagination, made us travel in time and space, and extended the confines of pop without losing sight of popularity. With the passing of time, rock music has changed, shedding its skin, so to speak, and reinventing itself time and again; it was a strange animal, a chimera, a dream, a hope, a desire that takes on different forms. So Bowie, with his multiple roles and personas, changed with the various seasons of rock with truly special agility and involvement. The Bowie of *Young Americans* is worlds away from the Bowie of *Tin Machine*, just as the person in *Space Oddity* is only remotely related to the one in *Heroes*.

But more than music was under Bowie's spell. Just try to imagine a world without Ziggy Stardust, or without the makeup, hair and costumes of Aladdin Sane. Our collective imagination would be drastically different indeed. Think of the cult of Berlin, a short time before the Wall fell,

which was celebrated in *Heroes* via an extreme, obscure, hard, stylized look. Then there's the rock 'n' roll culture of America represented on stage with the oversize jackets and wide trousers of *Young Americans*. One could say that many people, especially during the era of glam rock, platform shoes and abundant glitter, have paid tribute to Bowie without even knowing it, wearing clothes and accessories that in some way were created with him in their subconscious, and that many others in the mid-1970s were greatly influenced by the elegance of the *Thin White Duke*.

While many rock stars have created an intense, signature persona or image that has endured and changed the world of style and fashion, Bowie did so many times over, constantly transforming both his face and body. In so doing, he never followed a trend but rather created new ones. The worlds of art, cinema and fashion enthusiastically welcomed Bowie's influence, precisely because his constant metamorphoses tested the capacity of his observers to understand the complexity of life. Being like him was impossible, and even keeping up with his transformations was extremely difficult. 'I alone am Bowie,' he seemed to say every time a new record or project pushed his great creative imagination even further, 'killing' the latest persona to be reborn once again.

108   DAVID BOWIE IN A PHOTO TAKEN DURING A SESSION FOR THE COVER OF *PIN UPS* (1973).

The new image was never anything short of bold, believable and intense. The same held true even in the 1980s, when Bowie stopped his chameleon-like changes, becoming a style icon with a kind of elegance that no other famous rock star – from McCartney to Lou Reed, and not even Eric Clapton, a close friend of Armani – could dream of. Art and elegance, excess and extravagance, stylishness and fascination, they were all part and parcel of Bowie. He himself was always the focus of his creations, never separating the music from the image and always merging the various stylistic elements – visual, gestural and sound – into a single work of art.

And then there are the songs, each of them a gem from a single, infinite necklace, irreplaceable jewels that have left their indelible mark on the history of music. His fundamental albums have left their traces over time, making history, being at once both pop and avant-garde, electronic and soul, jungle and R&B, romantic and psychedelic, up to Bowie's 'last act': death, narrated in his unsurpassable masterpiece *Blackstar*, a song in which truth, life, death and art become one.

110-111 DAVID BOWIE ON STAGE AS THE THIN WHITE DUKE AT THE WEMBLEY EMPIRE POOL IN LONDON DURING THE 1976 PROMOTIONAL TOUR OF *STATION TO STATION*.

David Bowie

128

Singles released.

150

Number, in millions, of Bowie albums sold.

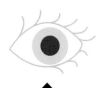

1947

David Bowie is born.

1967

David Bowie makes his recording debut.

1975

The year Bowie tops the charts for the first time in the U.S., with *Fame*, which he wrote and sang with John Lennon.

72

Videos produced
during Bowie's career.

10

Bands he worked with.

26

Number of studio
albums released
during his career.

4

Number of times his
Major Tom persona
appeared: three in the
songs *Space Oddity*,
Ashes to Ashes and *Hello
Spaceboy*, and once,
according to many
people, in the *Blackstar*
video.

Bowie's ranking on the
list of the wealthiest
rock artists in the
world.

1995

The year of Bowie's
first exhibition as a
painter.

1997

He launches his
online Bowienet service.

2016

The year Bowie died.

1987

Bowie plays Pontius
Pilate in *The Last
Temptation of Christ*,
directed by Martin
Scorsese.

Elton John

Sir Elton John is a showman. His lifestyle, performances and his clothes are proof. He's a showman and he behaves like one. And, of course, he's treated like one, especially by his countless faithful fans. Sir Elton earned his 'divine' status in almost 50 years of writing songs and performing, starting from when he founded his first band as a young man in the early 1960s, to the glorious present. Born on March 25, 1947, Reginald Kenneth Dwight (his real name) always believed that music was his life, and the great success he has enjoyed demonstrates that he made the right choice. Besides winning many Grammy Awards, Elton John has sold at least 250 million albums, and has had at least one hit on the English Top 40 charts every year from 1972 to 1996. We aren't talking about 'ditties' here: Sir Elton was and still is one of the greatest pop music songwriters, especially in the 1970s, with albums such as *Tumbleweed Connection, Madman Across the Water, Honky Chateau, Don't Shoot Me I'm Only the Piano Player*, and *Goodbye Yellow Brick Road*, which in many respects established the rules of modern pop, containing such memorable songs as *Rocket Man, Your Song, Daniel* and many others. But John certainly didn't stop in the 1970s. Since then, he has continued to write songs, release dozens of highly successful albums, collaborate with many other artists, and write soundtracks for numerous wonderful movies. Among his most recent works, mention must be made of his album and supporting tour with the great Leon Russell and, seventeen years after winning an Oscar for *Lion King*, the soundtrack for the animated Disney film *Gnomeo & Juliet*, which he also produced. And then there are the concerts, in which John performs the catalog of his greatest songs, often broadcast live around the world and watched by millions. Present-day pop owes a lot to Elton John, with his highly original singer-songwriter style in the 1970s, the way he combines rock innovations, his love of glamor and flamboyant productions, melody and tradition. Many stars today would not be where and what they are, were it not for his having paved the way many years ago by 'updating' pop with intelligence and courage, creativity and talent. And in spite of it all, these very gifts allow him to continue to give audiences shows that are still amazing, concerts in which his consummate skill as entertainer and singer once again shines and his songs — both the glorious classic and the new creations — stand out so brilliantly, confirming that if anyone deserves to be dubbed a knight of pop culture it is certainly, and only, Elton John.

114   AN ECCENTRIC, ENTERTAINING ELTON JOHN DURING A CONCERT AT MADISON SQUARE GARDEN, NEW YORK (1976).

115

Elton John

400,000

Digital downloads of *Rocket Man* that again, in 2018, earned him a gold certification from the British Phonographic Industry.

40,000

The estimated number of glasses John has collected, some of which are the most bizarre and glam in the history of pop.

1973

Rocket Man (I Think It's Going To Be a Long, Long Time), a single that would reach no. 2 in the UK and no. 6 in the USA, is released.

The album *Don't Shoot Me I'm Only the Piano Player*, a tribute to the French film director François Truffaut, is released.

1947

Reginald Kenneth Dwight, better known as (Sir) Elton John, is born in London.

1967

John tries to become the vocalist of King Crimson and Gentle Giant.

50

The states in America in which John has performed.

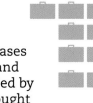

42

Number of suitcases full of clothes and accessories, divided by color, that he brought to Heathrow Airport in 1991, ready to take off.

3,500

Estimated minimum number of live Elton John concerts.

700

Minimum number of songs he has composed and released via 33 albums (plus three live albums and 14 compilations).

50

The songs by John that have been in the top 40 of English and American charts.

1975

By himself, Elton John accounts for over 2% of record sales worldwide.

1994

Elton John is inducted into the Rock and Roll Hall of Fame.

1998

Elton John is knighted by Queen Elizabeth II, becoming a Knight Bachelor.

2008

John auctions two of his grand pianos: a Steinway made of burr-maplewood, and a black Steinway built especially for his Beverly Hills mansion.

9

Albums that were consecutively no. 1 on the American charts.

3

Age when John began to play the piano.

Michael Jackson

A fairytale turned nightmare. Perhaps an apt description of Michael Jackson's career. A story of glory and decline that has few equals in American show business. Michael Jackson began his adventure in the entertainment world as a child wonder, together with his siblings Jackie, Tito, Jermaine, Marlon and Randy (who replaced Jermaine), the famous Jackson 5 that, after a long 'apprenticeship' under the guidance of their father Joe in Gary, Indiana, rapidly rose to stardom in the late 1960s. In 1969 they released their first album for Motown Records, *I Want You Back*, defined by the voice of a very young Michael. Over the next ten years, the Jackson brothers released 19 more albums, including official records, anthologies and special albums, and even appeared on TV with a cartoon. But the real star was little Michael, a gifted boy with an extraordinary voice and a cute, mischievous look who slowly grew up and began to think on his own. In 1978 he acted in *The Wiz* with Diana Ross, even singing on the film's soundtrack. The following year was Jackson's 'great leap forward': he left his brothers to get a taste of his first great solo success with *Off the Wall*, an album produced by Quincy Jones. This marked the beginning of a totally different project, one in which Jackson had total control of his 'product'. From that moment on, he called all the shots concerning his records, from the cover art to the songs, and his shows, from the set design to the choreography, including the 'moonwalk', the dance move that made him famous. This new strategy paid off,

and in 1982 Jackson conquered the entertainment world with his album *Thriller*, which, according to some estimates, has sold more than 100 million copies to this day. Also produced by Quincy Jones, it soon became one of the best-selling albums in the history of popular music, a disc that had all the right ingredients to please just about every audience you can think of, regardless of race, gender or age. With *Thriller* (masterfully directed by John Landis), Jackson initiated the era of long form videos that were more than just concert footage, producing famous clips that made a major contribution to the growth of this genre. Some have even become true classics (*Billie Jean* is another example). Jackson was now the most popular star in the world (along with Madonna), and Michaelmania, a term purposely created to compare the Jackson phenomenon with that of the Beatles 20 years earlier, spread like wildfire. After the landslide success of *Thriller*, earning Jackson seven Grammy Awards, his fans had to wait until 1987 for another album. Sadly, his comeback coincided with a disturbing metamorphosis: oceanic success had transformed a once-cheerful Michael into a megalomaniac, egocentric, capricious star weighed down by phobias. He even went so far as to change his face, and perhaps the color of his skin, through plastic surgery. As a result, his 'stage mask' was now permanently engraved on his face. And although both *Bad* (1987) and *Dangerous* (1991) sold dozens of millions of copies, nothing came close to the success of his first album.

118 A YOUNG MICHAEL JACKSON ON STAGE AT THE ROSEMONT HORIZON IN ILLINOIS (APRIL 1988).

The Michael Jackson legend began to weaken, as the triumph of rap pushed him to the margins of black music, and the rise of boy bands made him less popular with white teenagers. Jackson found himself entirely unable to deal with such a crisis. Matters worsened in 1993, when he was first accused of child molestation. Jackson therefore decided to present himself in a different light. In 1994 he married Elvis Presley's daughter, Lisa Marie, but they soon divorced, and in 1996 he married Debbie Rowe, who became the mother of his two children. Despite his antics, Jackson's worldwide success had come to an end. Albums and compilations followed one another without real impact, rumors of bankruptcy became increasingly vociferous, and by the late 1990s Michaelmania was a distant memory. Success and the charts had eluded him, and in the final years of his life the media seemed to be interested only in the legal troubles of the former child prodigy, who for ten years had been the indisputable King of Pop. In the next decade, bankruptcy arrived and Jackson, who had even purchased the rights to the Beatles catalog, now found himself forced to sell everything, including his legendary Neverland Ranch in California. More accusations of pedophilia and more courtroom acquittals followed. But things could never go back to how they were.

Before his death in June 2009, Jackson had been planning a big comeback, one last extreme attempt to regain the throne that he had lost, and perhaps regain that part of himself lost to the shadow of fame and fortune.

Michael Jackson

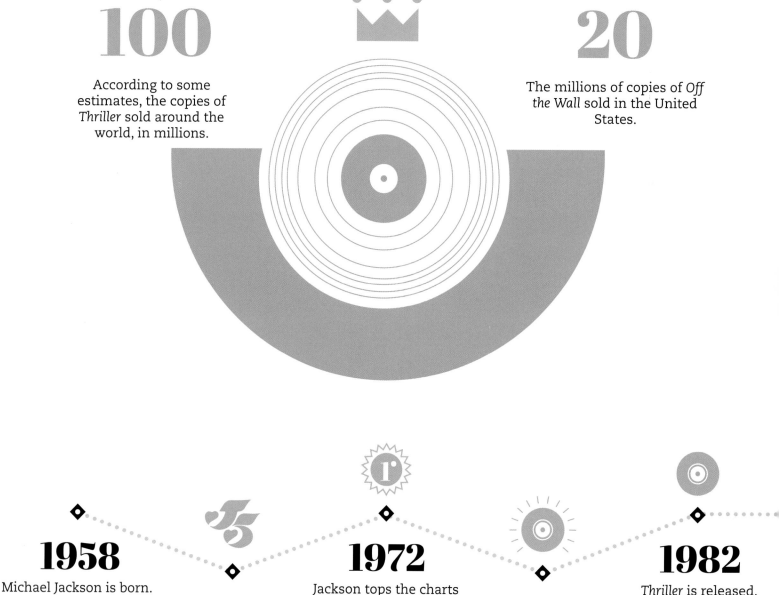

100

According to some estimates, the copies of *Thriller* sold around the world, in millions.

20

The millions of copies of *Off the Wall* sold in the United States.

1958

Michael Jackson is born.

1969

The first Jackson 5 single, *I Want You Back*, is released.

1972

Jackson tops the charts with his single *Ben*.

1979

Jackson makes his debut as a solo artist with *Off the Wall*.

1982

Thriller is released.

11

The runtime, in minutes, of the video for *Black or White*.

5

The singles taken from the album *Bad* that peaked at no.1 in the American charts.

5

Little Michael's age when he began to sing with his brothers.

1

Position (no. 1) that *Billie Jean* achieved contemporaneously on the pop and R&B singles charts as *Thriller* on the charts of pop and R&B albums.

1985

Jackson writes *We Are the World* with Lionel Richie.

2002

Jackson is photographed while dangling his nine-month-old son over the edge of a balcony.

2003

Accusations of sexually molesting a twelve year-old boy are lodged.

2005

Jackson is acquitted of the accusation.

2009

Jackson dies in Los Angeles.

Coldplay

Chris Martin is not a rock star. He's the former classmate that everyone wants to run into after so many years, the friend who never forgets your birthday, the big brother who listens to you when you have a problem, the guy who sings what you would like to sing in moments of joy and even when in times of intense melancholy. He's a pop icon with Coldplay, and when he's on stage, he transforms. For years, Coldplay has managed, more than any other band, to express that curious sentiment that combines sadness and happiness, and then very gradually changes with time, turning that sadness into feelings of hope, love of life, a whirlwind of positive emotions. Coldplay is pop, dance and rock, but most of all the band contains everything necessary to remind us that life still exists on planet Earth. Coldplay has exactly what every music lover desires: intelligence, profundity, joy and warmth, accompanied by tempo, research into sound, songwriting, melody, rhythm, and dance, as well as electronica, rock, ballads and emotions. This is the art of pop at its peak, its apex, its quintessence. Incredibly, every album is different from the next, as if the band is searching for the perfect pop song. They proceed by trial and error, and each trial leads them closer to the goal – music in color. Some will remark that music has always been in color. Cinema got there along the way, television a long time afterward, while music has always been in color, enhancing he hues of the rainbow in their splendid immateriality, their marvelous non-existence. But Coldplay goes even further, using technique to create a kaleidoscope, shifting into Technicolor overdrive. Their music verges on fantasy to create worlds and stories, as well as to narrate life, something that Chris Martin does systematically with his songs. A comparison with the Beatles wouldn't be exaggerated. Coldplay's ambition is similar; the desire to astonish and at the same time move people is the same. Both bands have the conviction that you can't just keep repeating the same formula and that you must speak to the hearts of a broad public. Moreover, one phrase encapsulates the philosophy of both the Beatles and Coldplay: "all you need is love." That should be enough to make the comparison well-founded.

124-125 COLDPLAY WITH FRONTMAN, SONGWRITER AND VOCALIST CHRIS MARTIN, ON STAGE DURING THE ITUNES FESTIVAL AT THE ROUNDHOUSE IN LONDON ON 22 JULY 2011.

Coldplay

15,000

The amount paid, in pounds, for Johnny Buckland's guitar at a charity auction.

4.22

Amount spent, in millions of pounds, to give the members of their audiences luminous bracelets.

55

Millions of albums sold.

12

Albums released.

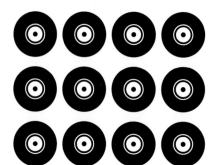

9

Video streams, in millions, of *Something Just Like This* in only 24 hours.

1998

The first Coldplay EP, *Safety*, is released.

1996

The our musicians meet at University College London.

2000

Coldplay's debut album *Parachutes* is released.

122

Number of concerts in the band's *A Head Full of Dreams* tour (2017).

107

The number of awards the band has won.

29

Grammy nominations.

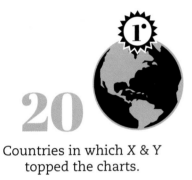

20

Countries in which X & Y topped the charts.

7

Grammy Awards won.

5

Chris Martin's age when he began playing piano.

2008

The band begins its collaboration with Brian Eno.

2011

The year of the *Princess of China* duet with Rihanna.

Amy Winehouse

Winehouse died when she was only twenty-seven. Just like Brian Jones in 1969, Jimi Hendrix and Janis Joplin in 1970, Jim Morrison in 1971, Kurt Cobain in 1994, and so many others. Twenty-seven years of music, but also drugs, alcohol, and pushing the limits. Twenty-seven years in which they became some of the most beloved stars in music, broke all the rules, tore down barriers and ended their lives and careers prematurely. Like Icarus, burned by a desire to overcome every limit and to experience, physically and theoretically, the absolutely extreme limit of life itself. Turing twenty-seven is a sort of curse, a point of no return for those in the 27 Club who, while seeking their own eternity, were not even able to grow, to become true adults and pass from one phase of life to another. Some might say that the fault lies with rock music, its 'golden rule' of 'sex, drugs and rock 'n' roll. But such a simplification doesn't do justice to the countless other artists who came well before rock and ruined their lives and potential all the same – poets, painters and composers of every generation. Besides, Amy Winehouse wasn't a rock artist. Her music was based on blues and her fate could, at most, have been the same as Billie Holiday's, though the latter lived much longer. Furthermore, times have changed, and the aura that surrounded the death of Hendrix, Morrison and Joplin – all unable to deal with normality – has given way to an overall sobriety and a different interpretation of 'divinity' in rock music (for example, Bono and Bruce Spingsteen), or to

a sort of self-control that convinced even those whose lifestyle was based on excess, such as Keith Richards or David Crosby, to reach the age of retirement in the best possible condition. There is nothing poetic, rebellious or romantic about these wasted lives. Nor is there the fascination of an inner search taken to its extreme consequences. There is only solitude, the dissipation of talent and energy, and the waste of a gift that led them not only to dream, but to create art that is downright unforgettable. We are left with regret and sorrow over the loss of artists who, instead of destroying their lives, could have kept illuminating the world. We are also left with great, brilliant sounds, Jimi's piercing guitar, Jim's shout. And the crooning of Amy, who in a few short years left her mark on music, a mark that will never be erased by time. Amy Winehouse loved soul and blues, as well as Jamaican music and jazz. She had a prodigious talent and is without a doubt the most important female singer of the third millennium. Her voice changed the rules of the game, it imposed a new style of singing, which female vocalists everywhere have tried to imitate. Creative, anguished, overwhelming, passionate, elusive and nonconformist, Amy Winehouse released just two albums, *Frank* and *Back to Black*, which changed the destiny of pop. As a songwriter and singer she injected an incredibly huge dose of truth into music, putting it where it belonged, forgetting about marketing and the music industry and thinking only of expression and art. It's almost impossible to imagine music today without her.

128 A FINE PORTRAIT OF AMY WINEHOUSE, WHO DIED ON JULY 23, 2011, TAKEN TO PROMOTE *AMY*, A BIOGRAPHICAL MOVIE DIRECTED BY ASIF KAPADIA.

Amy Winehouse

209,000

The number of copies of *Back to Black* sold in only one week in December 2007.

82

Weeks that Winehouse's albums were in the British Top Ten.

2

Back to Black is the second best-selling album in the 21st century in England. The first is Adele's 21.

3

The Ivor Novello Awards Winehouse won (2004, 2007 and 2008).

2003

Winehouse's first album, *Frank*, is released.

2007

Winehouse and Blake Fielder-Civil get married.

2007

Winehouse is arrested in Bergen, Norway for marijuana possession.

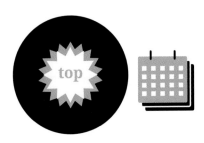

19

Consecutive weeks *Rehab* was in the Top Ten.

5

Grammy Awards won in 2008.

2009

Winehouse and Blake Fielder-Civil get divorced.

2009

Winehouse starts her own record label, Lioness Records.

2010

The Amy Winehouse for Fred Perry collection is created.

2011

The year Winehouse dies.

Punk

1977: while the streets of London were being decorated to celebrate Queen Elizabeth's Silver Jubilee, the Sex Pistols released their first, revolutionary single, *God Save the Queen*. It was a slap in the face to English institutions and, at the same time, a sensational gesture against the rock establishment, a small bomb that exploded in the heart of British music to make it clear that something had changed. 1977 marked a new era-defining turning point in youth culture. In Europe, it took on the shape of a new political rebellion, terrorism and independence from the old political status quo. In England and America, it was transformed into music, a lifestyle, the open contestation of all rules: this, was punk. From 1975 to 1979, punk was the new global phenomenon. It was the last major, historic rock explosion. Very short, brightly-dyed hair, safety pins stuck just about everywhere, leather jackets and ripped jeans became the 'uniform' of a new army of desperate, rebellious young people who no longer wanted anything to do with the establishment and wanted to live "outside society," as Patti Smith sang. Music in the mid-1970s had witnessed the triumph of regimented, overplayed disco - the opium of the proletariat, an agent of social order, as punk exponents yelled - as well as album-

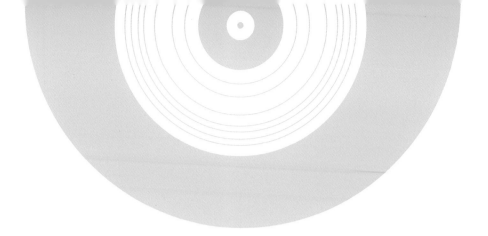

oriented radio and colossal progressive bands detached from reality and street life. Punk came into being in order to regain possession of a musical language that seemed destined to be confused for good. It was a subculture that quickly attracted the attention of the media, a cultural phenomenon that imposed a lifestyle all its own. But it didn't come out of nowhere. When everything is said and done, punk has always existed, ingrained in rock. It is an attitude and posturing of music, its rebellion and electricity, that refuses to be conditioned by anything but itself. The Who of *My Generation*, the Rolling Stones of *Let It Bleed*, the 13th Floor Elevators and the Lingsmen, Pretty Things, and Electric Prunes were punk. Hard, harsh sounds connected to the slums, mixed with the coarse music-making of juvenile bands, vivacious subcultures, and teenagers searching for an identity. England is customarily considered the birthplace of punk as we know it today, conceived by artistic agitator and band manager Malcolm McLaren, fashion designer Vivienne Westwood, and the notes of a seedy and outrageous band like Johnny Rotten and Sid Vicious' Sex Pistols. And it generated great personalities such as the members of the Clash, Siouxsie and the Banshees, the Stranglers and, in the United States, Patti Smith, Richard Hell, and the Ramones. It was short-lived, a flame that burned with incredible intensity. After which rock was never the same again.

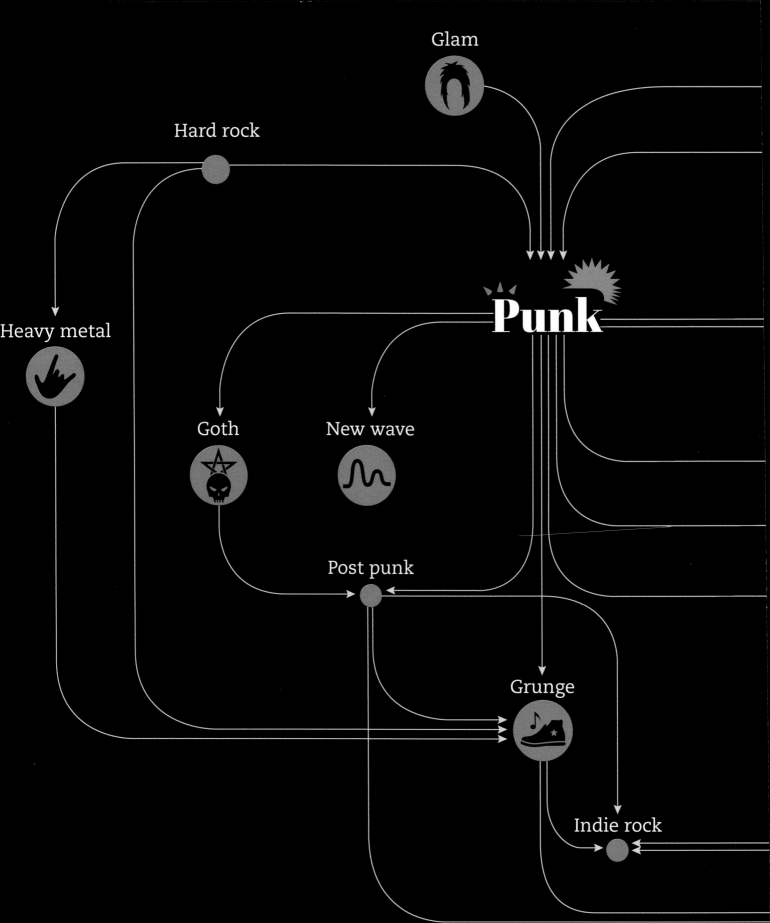

Glam

Hard rock

Heavy metal

Punk

Goth

New wave

Post punk

Grunge

Indie rock

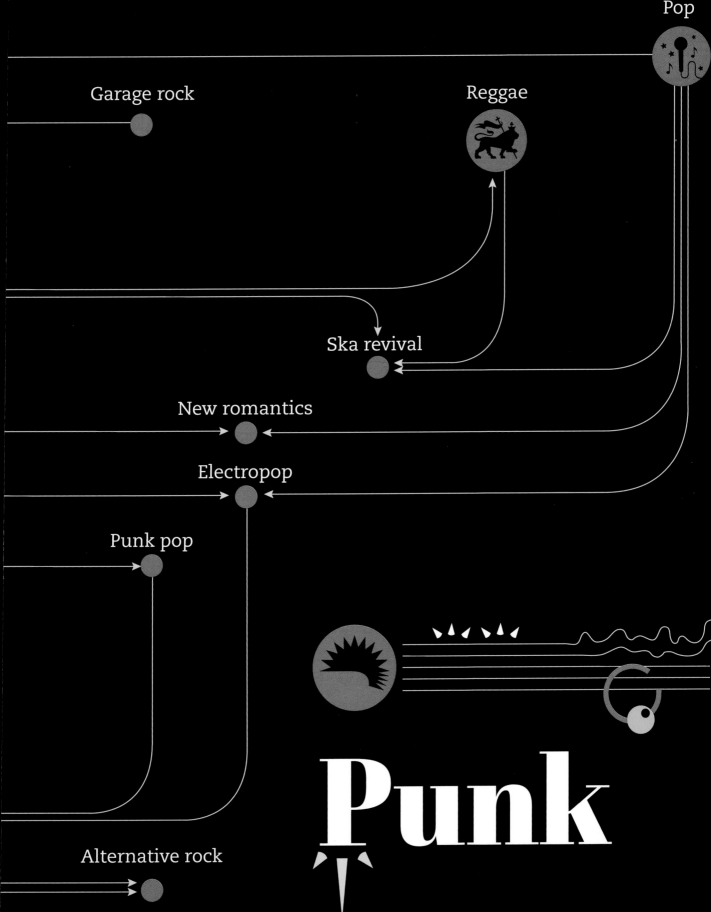

Pop

Garage rock

Reggae

Ska revival

New romantics

Electropop

Punk pop

Punk

Alternative rock

Ramones

A little more than 40 years ago, the Ramones, with their altered rock 'n' roll, leather jackets and high-speed and hyper-electric songs, became, together with the Sex Pistols in England, the symbol of a musical and cultural revolution whose echoes still resound: punk. At its core, the band's music was never true punk; its sonic universe was rock 'n' roll, surf, the music that bridged the late 1950s and early 1960s. But it was the members' behavior that distinguished them from all other bands in the mid-1970s. In fact, they were the exact opposites of their contemporaries. They wanted entertainment and chaos, electricity and energy, to be the core of their music, with songs based on three or four chords, performed on stage without fuss, quite the opposite of typical rock star behavior. They were music from the street that emerged from stereos in cars driven by rebellious adolescents who were fed up with hippies and progressive music, easy listening and pop. They were four 'brothers' dressed alike in leather jackets and torn jeans. And they wanted to play nothing but brief, fast-paced songs, one after the other, in order to make the audiences go wild and get crazy, the only 'pause' between the songs being the magic formula of "one, two, three, four." Johnny, Dee Dee, Joey and Tommy. Their story lasted 22 years, from their debut at Forest Hills in 1974, through an epic season of concerts held at CBGB's and Max's Kansas City, up to their world conquest and then their definitive break-up in 1996 – after having played 2,263 concerts and recorded fourteen albums. But it was the infinite cultural impact of the 'fast four' that has allowed the band to survive even after the original members have left us. The 'Ramone Brothers' had become an integral part of the collective imagination, an indestructible icon of rock 'n' roll, the image of intensity, entertainment, rebellion and energy in music that emerges from its ashes every time it seems to have died. The Ramones were not only punk. Like fleet-footed torch bearers, they ran the flame lit by Elvis into the 1990s, passing it on to the rockers of successive generations. And they are still extremely popular, and certainly not because of nostalgia. One often sees adolescents wearing Ramones t-shirts, which are sold in outlets and chain stores for young people, because their still-popular songs are ageless. Even the cover of *Road to Ruin* depicts them as comic strip characters, icons of the collective imagination, more like Mickey Mouse or Superman than dusty old rock stars.

137   THE RAMONES PHOTOGRAPHED ON A NEW YORK STREET IN THE 1970S.

138   JOEY RAMONE PERFORMING AT THE HAMMERSMITH ODEON IN OCTOBER 1978.

Ramones

2,263

Number of concerts the fast four played from 1974 to 1996, an average of two per week.

6,400

Dollars invested in the production of their debut album, *Ramones*, which was eventually went gold in the U.S. and became the immortal icon of this influential band.

315

The number on Bowery Street, New York City of the mythical punk/new wave music club CBGB opened in 1973. The Ramones debuted here and it became the permanent venue for their live performances.

50

Number of times Phil Spector made Johnny repeat the introduction of *Rock 'n' Roll High School*, the beginning of the soundtrack of the movie of the same name (1979), also on the album *End of the Century* (1980).

10

According to Legs McNeil, the future co-founder of *Punk* magazine, this was the maximum number of spectators in the audience.

4

Number of band members, always.

4

People who replaced the original drum and bass musicians, Tommy and Dee Dee, all of whom used the Ramone pseudonym.

0

Original band members who are still alive.

1974

The year of the birth of the quartet that became the symbol of American punk.

1989

Pet Sematary is released, a song based on Stephen King's novel of the same name and then added to the soundtrack of the novel's inevitable movie version.

Sex Pistols

One album alone, *Never Mind the Bollocks*, was sufficient for the Sex Pistols to join the rock pantheon, part of more than 60 years of history that was shocked, to say the least, when this band first appeared. Only one album and three years of activity were needed for the Sex Pistols to become one of the most important bands in rock history, regardless of their musical qualities, success, and whether or not one likes punk. The band was formed in 1975 in a clothing shop in Chelsea run by Malcolm McLaren and Vivienne Westwood. But it was in 1977, while the streets of London were being decorated for Queen Elizabeth's Silver Jubilee, that the Sex Pistols released their first, revolutionary single, a track that went straight to the heart of British traditions and scandalized conventional, 'right-minded' citizens. Splashed across the front page of every major newspaper, the song was *God Save the Queen* and it brought punk to the world. 'No Future' was the movement's simple, immediate and direct slogan, encapsulating everything behind of a form of music that arose in the mid-1970s and shook the rock star system to its foundations. No future, no hope, no desire: the teenagers in the limelight in the mid-1970s had not grown up with the dreams of the decade before them. Those dreams were over and done, a distant memory, and besides, these youngsters didn't want to change the world. They knew the world couldn't be changed, so they decided to shout angrily, with outrage and violence, about their need to exist. Punk was the rock 'n' roll of a generation without hopes and dreams that saw no possibility of a better future and consequently set out to express its rage unabashedly

140 THE SEX PISTOLS, AUTHORS OF *THE GREAT ROCK 'N' ROLL SWINDLE* AND THE 'FATHERS' OF ENGLISH PUNK. FROM LEFT, SID VICIOUS, JOHNNY ROTTEN, STEVE JONES AND PAUL COOK.

141 A POSTER FROM THE SEX PISTOLS' CONCERT AT THE 100 CLUB ON OXFORD STREET, LONDON.

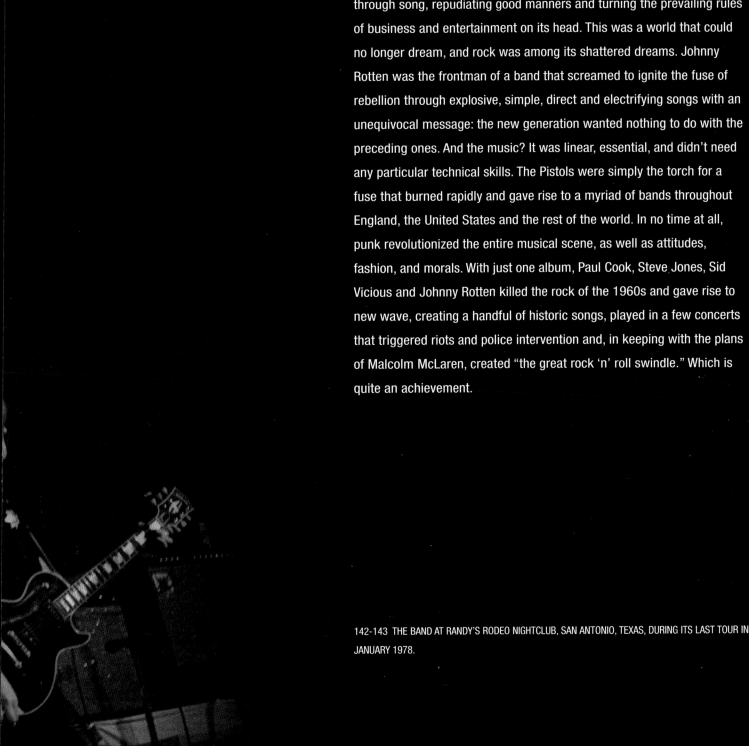

through song, repudiating good manners and turning the prevailing rules of business and entertainment on its head. This was a world that could no longer dream, and rock was among its shattered dreams. Johnny Rotten was the frontman of a band that screamed to ignite the fuse of rebellion through explosive, simple, direct and electrifying songs with an unequivocal message: the new generation wanted nothing to do with the preceding ones. And the music? It was linear, essential, and didn't need any particular technical skills. The Pistols were simply the torch for a fuse that burned rapidly and gave rise to a myriad of bands throughout England, the United States and the rest of the world. In no time at all, punk revolutionized the entire musical scene, as well as attitudes, fashion, and morals. With just one album, Paul Cook, Steve Jones, Sid Vicious and Johnny Rotten killed the rock of the 1960s and gave rise to new wave, creating a handful of historic songs, played in a few concerts that triggered riots and police intervention and, in keeping with the plans of Malcolm McLaren, created "the great rock 'n' roll swindle." Which is quite an achievement.

142-143 THE BAND AT RANDY'S RODEO NIGHTCLUB, SAN ANTONIO, TEXAS, DURING ITS LAST TOUR IN JANUARY 1978.

40,000

The payment, in pounds, stipulated in the band's first contract with EMI.

13

Albums in the band's official discography to this day, including twelve that are either live or compilations.

9

Solo albums by Sid Vicious, all of which were posthumous.

1975

The year of the birth of the band, revolutionizing the world of rock (and not only).

1977

Bassist Glen Matlock is replaced by Sid Vicious, the true punk icon.

God Save the Queen reaches 2nd place on the official English charts and tops the *New Musical Express* chart.

1978

On October 12, Nancy Spungen dies of an abdominal knife wound while staying in a hotel with her inseparable boyfriend Sid Vicious, who is accused of homicide.

1979

Sid Vicious dies of heroin overdose, becoming yet another member of the ill-fated rock star pantheon.

6 The day in November 1976 when the band first performed at the Central Saint Martins College of Art and Design of London, which marked the 'official' beginning of punk.

4 Band members: Steve Jones, Paul Cook, Sid Vicious (pseudonym of John Simon Ritchie) and Johnny Rotten (pseudonym of John Lydon).

3 The band's career actually lasted only three years.

1 The album *Never Mind Bollocks, Here's the Sex Pistols* made the band famous and is in fact the only studio album the group recorded.

1980

The docufiction film *The Great Rock and Roll Swindle*, directed by Julian Temple, is released.

1986

The year *Sid & Nancy* is released, directed by Alex Cox and based on the tragic story of Sid Vicious and his girlfriend Nancy Spungen.

1996

The Sex Pistols reunite (with Glen Matlock as bassist) for the Filthy Lucre World Tour, which lasts six months and includes concerts in Europe, North and South America, Australia and Japan.

2006

In keeping with their (profitable) myth, the Sex Pistols scornfully refuse to be inducted to the Rock and Roll Hall of 'Shame' (as they call it).

The Clash

If it is true that the dream of rock 'n' roll is to make raw, rebellious music that communicates with the young in their language and mirrors their energy, that has the strength needed to describe life with few words and guitar chords and thus express, simply and passionately, the desires, anxiety and rage of generations of adolescents around the world, then there is no doubt that this type of music has been embodied most of all by the Clash. The band – Joe Strummer, Mick Jones, Paul Simonon, and Topper Headon – epitomized the sound and image of a youthful myth that refuses to die, of music that needs nothing else but passion, energy and power to keep pace with the world and everyday life. Out of tune, abrasive guitars and songs sung tensely: this was the simple and effective formula that the Clash always offered, playing the role of the world's last rock 'n' roll heroes, the heirs of the most rigorous punk music, in which immediacy and spontaneity triumph over technique. But the Clash is so much more. Its members are supporters of the down and out, experimenters of rhythm and funk, unabashed rebels who singing against every form of injustice, abuse of power and repression as well as in favor of hopes and dreams for a better world. Joe Strummer led this 'gang of desperados' of rock 'n' roll, playing memorable songs in a captivating yet chaotic manner, combining punk and reggae, dub and soul, in a musical adventure that lasted exactly ten years, from 1976 to 1986, ten years in which they produced such masterful albums as *The Clash, London Calling* and *Sandinista*. Together with the Sex Pistols, they were the protagonists of the English punk explosion, despite the fact that only one of their albums, the first, could reasonably be placed in that category. They were always punk at heart, even later, when their 'combat rock' became multifarious and multicolored, but their style – three chords and so much rhythm – was not sufficient for a band that set out to conquer the world and revive rock. So, with only a handful of records in a very short period, the Clash fought with the weapons at its disposal, telling stories about street life and broken dreams, epitomizing the rebellious spirit of rock 'n' roll – libertarian and relentless, made of gold and dust – that has been with us for almost 60 years, experimenting with reggae, punk, funk, soul and rock 'n' roll, in a marvelous kaleidoscope of inconceivable power. Joe Strummer, the driving force of a legendary band that is still adored and respected, is no longer with us, but the sound of the Clash is still here, in the sound of the new millennium.

146 THE COVER OF THE CLASH'S SINGLE *COMPLETE CONTROL*, RELEASED IN 1977.

147 THE CLASH IN A PHOTO TAKEN IN 1982. FROM LEFT: MICK JONES, TOPPER HEADON, JOE STRUMMER AND PAUL SIMONON.

THE CLASH

 48

The hours, later reduced to 24, that the band's manager gave Strummer to decide to leave the 101ers and agree to become the lead vocalist of the newly-formed Clash.

19

The tracks of their absolute masterpiece, *London Calling*, the double album with the immortal cover featuring Paul Simonon destroying his Fender Precision Bass at the Palladium in New York City (September 20, 1979). The bass is now kept in the Rock and Roll Hall of Fame in Cleveland.

1976

The year the Clash was officially formed, making its debut as the supporting band for the Sex Pistols during their Anarchy Tour.

1977

English punk explodes with a mythical triad: *White Riot*, *Complete Control* and *Clash City Rockers*. Strummer and Jones are arrested for a number of misdemeanors, from vandalism to marijuana possession and even stealing a pillowcase, and Simonon and Headon for having shot at pigeons with a compressed air rifle.

1985

Joe Strummer records the last Clash album (*Cut The Crap*), with only one member of the original quartet, Simonon, while Mick Jones leaves the band and forms Big Audio Dynamite (B.A.D).

That same year, the Clash signs a contract with CBS and is accused of selling out.

1986

Strummer writes the songs for *Sid & Nancy*, the film directed by Alex Cox.

10

Total number of band members. Besides the original lineup with Joe Strummer, Paul Simonon (bass), Mick Jones (guitar), and Topper Headon (percussion), there were three guitarists and three drummers who alternated with the above members at both the beginning and end of the quartet's career.

12

Total number of albums Joe Strummer created without The Clash, six of which are soundtracks.

1989

Strummer appears in Jim Jarmusch's *Mystery Train* in the role of a drunkard.

Lorem ipsum

2002

Joe Strummer dies of a heart attack.

2019

Former Clash guitarist Mick Jones makes a surprise comeback as a narrator in the studio recording of the promised new Flaming Lips album, *King's Mouth*.

 ## 3

Number of records in the band's best release, *Sandinista* (1980), an album with proto-rap elements.

50 GREEN DAY, THE MOST FAMOUS AMERICAN POP PUNK BAND FROM THE 1990S; FROM LEFT: MIKE DIRNT, BILLIE JOE ARMSTRONG AND TRE COOL.

52 GREEN DAY GUITARIST AND VOCALIST, BILLIE JOE ARMSTRONG, WHO HAS WRITTEN MOST OF THE BAND'S SONGS.

Green Day

Punk, original punk, that is, was born around 1976. Present-day punk, on the other hand, may have originated exactly ten years later, when Green Day was formed in Berkeley, California. Other dates certainly could mark the birth of this style, but there is no doubt that Green Day — that is, Billie Joe Armstrong, Tré Cool and Mike Dirnt, as well as Jason White, who has been playing with them since 1997 — have been, and still are, the most successful punk band from the 1990s on. For these young Americans, punk is an attitude, a way of life, and by no means a musical genre, given the technical prowess, studio production and sound of the band, which are decidedly more 'refined' than those of punk's forefathers. They've gone for something caustic, fast-paced, immediate, electric and wiry, purposely fashioned to make listeners feel immersed in a vibrant bustle of rebellious sensations and feelings. One could, and perhaps should, say that for Green Day, punk is more of an excuse than a reality. Perhaps what it needed (as is true of many other bands belonging to this punk 'rebirth') was the chance to feel like it was elsewhere, even with respect to grunge and alternative, in a small, recognizable universe in which fun and chaos could still get along. To do so, they brought punk into pop, into the international musical mainstream, by mixing melodies, refrains and songs with rhythm and explosive sound. So, there is much more to it than the list of three-minute songs in the band's long discography. Of course, it's a discography that boasts some masterpieces, such as *Dookie* (1994), a record-breaking album that sold 15 million copies, won a Grammy, and by itself would be enough to place Green Day at the peak of late 20th-century rock, and *American Idiot* (2004), a perfect example of how the band matured both musically and in terms of content. No longer mere rebellion and enjoyment, but commitment and consciousness, translated into songs that embody the contemporary scene in an essential, passionate way.

Billy Joe Armstrong has had a complicated personal life and went through a period of drug addiction, which he got over with great determination. The band has had alternating phases of great creativity and moments of reflection, but has always managed to remain not only at the top of the charts, but above all in the hearts of their fans, partly thanks to a live show that is absolutely explosive, full of energy, overwhelming, and fresh.

Green Day

15

Copies, in millions, of *Dookie* sold worldwide. It is still Green Day's best-selling album, and most probably the most successful 'punk' album of all from an economic standpoint.

 6

Age of (future) Green Day bassist Mike Dirnt when he was taken from his drug addicted mother and entrusted to a foster family.

10 ⬤

Armstrong's age when his father died of cancer, the tragic event of his childhood that inspired his composition of *Wake Me up When September Ends.*

3

Skulls on the cover of *Insomniac*, the third of which is difficult to make out. In fact, it is on the lower right among the flames and must be viewed from an angle, much like the anamorphic skull in Hans Holbein's famous Renaissance painting *The Ambassadors.*

33

The 'age' of the band, which was formed in 1986.

15 ⌂

Mike Dirnt's age when he left home to live with Billie Joe Armstrong.

5

The number of true hit singles on the album *Dookie*, the best 'quintet' of songs produced by the California trio: *Longview, Basket Case, Welcome to Paradise, When I Come around* and *She.*

◆ **1995**

The year Green Day vocalist Billie Joe considered leaving the band, as he was anxiety-ridden by the idea of having to repeat the success of the band's preceding album, *Dookie.*

◆ **2001**

Armstrong is robbed at gunpoint. Since then, he has allegedly been terrorized by weapons, a feeling reinforced by the non-violent spirit that has always characterized the band.

Hard & Heavy

At a certain point rock, became 'hard rock'. Actually, it may have always been that way. What other word would you use to define the riffs of the Kinks, the Who, Hendrix or certain harsh passages played by the Rolling Stones? Yet the fact remains that toward the end of the 1960s rock tended to simplify its approach, raise the volume of the amps, focus on vigorous drumming and decide that 'when the game gets tough, the tough begin to play'. Hard rock was born when a part of rock seemed to be abandoning its strident elements and simplicity in favor of research. This marked the first major split in the rock world, the separation between progressive and hard rock, between those who wanted to break off from the rock 'establishment' and those who wanted to remain solidly anchored to it.

To simplify matters, Black Sabbath, Deep Purple and Led Zeppelin are said to be the at the root of the 'hard' sound, each in its own way, obviously, and each with its own sound and ideas. But upon closer inspection, the only true fathers of a new 'genre' were Black Sabbath, who established the rules and language of something that went far beyond classical hard rock. While Deep Purple flirted with and then accepted progressive rock, and Led Zeppelin became masters of blues rock, Black Sabbath had nothing at all to do with either. Instead, they generated a precise, dark, aggressive, super-amplified and extremely solid sound that was no longer just 'hard', but also 'heavy' and relentless.

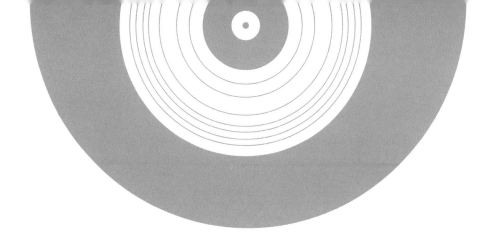

There are various versions of how the term 'heavy metal' came to be. The most literary one belongs to William Burroughs, who was the first to use this term in *The Soft Machine* in 1962; the most musical one is in the soundtrack of the film *Easy Rider* (1968) and in Steppenwolf's *Born to Be Wild*, which speaks of their "heavy metal thunder"; the third, which has more to do with music criticism, insists that the first person to use this term as a musical category was journalist Lester Bangs, in 1971.

Heavy metal has a sound, a look, a universe of references made up of signs and gestures, books and movies, whereas hard rock often lies at the exact opposite pole of the 'accursed' image of heavy metal - case in point: AC/DC. Heavy metal became the rampart of the 'defenders' of rock in the 1980s, the period when rock, after the explosion of punk, was overwhelmed by new wave and electronic instruments.

Heavy metal was one of the driving forces of the last great wave of rock in the 1990s, through grunge and alternative; it was the means by which rock succeeded in entering the universe of hip hop thanks to bands that ingeniously made the crossover between these two worlds. It survived trends and the record industry crisis, remaining basically the same, creating a host of subgenres, remaining a vital, youthful scene connected to the street and to life - a sound for those who consider themselves intransigent, who stoically resist the rules of 'normal' life and know quite well that a shout is at times louder than a bomb.

Hard & Heavy

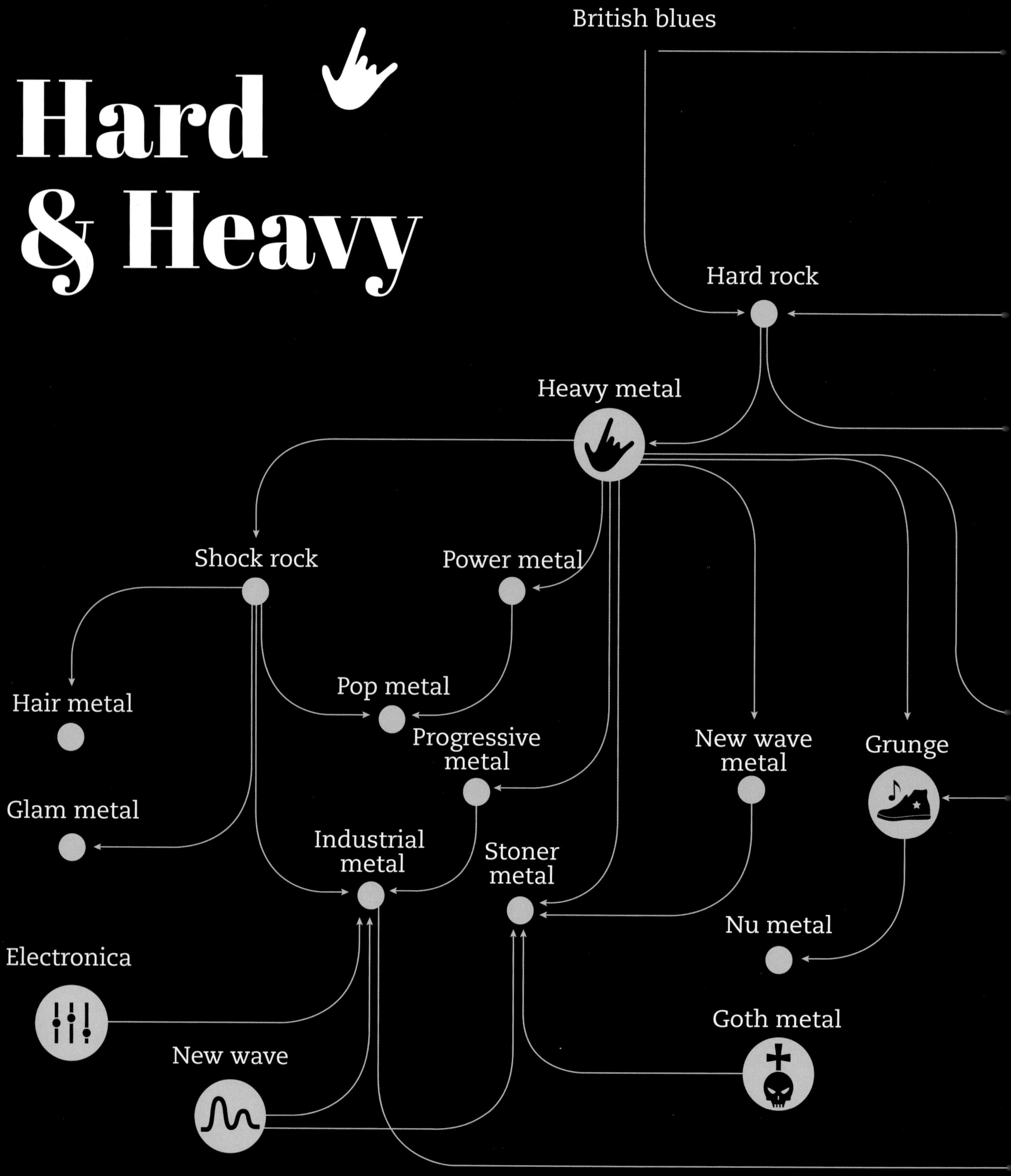

British blues

Hard rock

Heavy metal

Shock rock

Power metal

Hair metal

Pop metal

Glam metal

Progressive metal

Industrial metal

Stoner metal

New wave metal

Grunge

Nu metal

Electronica

Goth metal

New wave

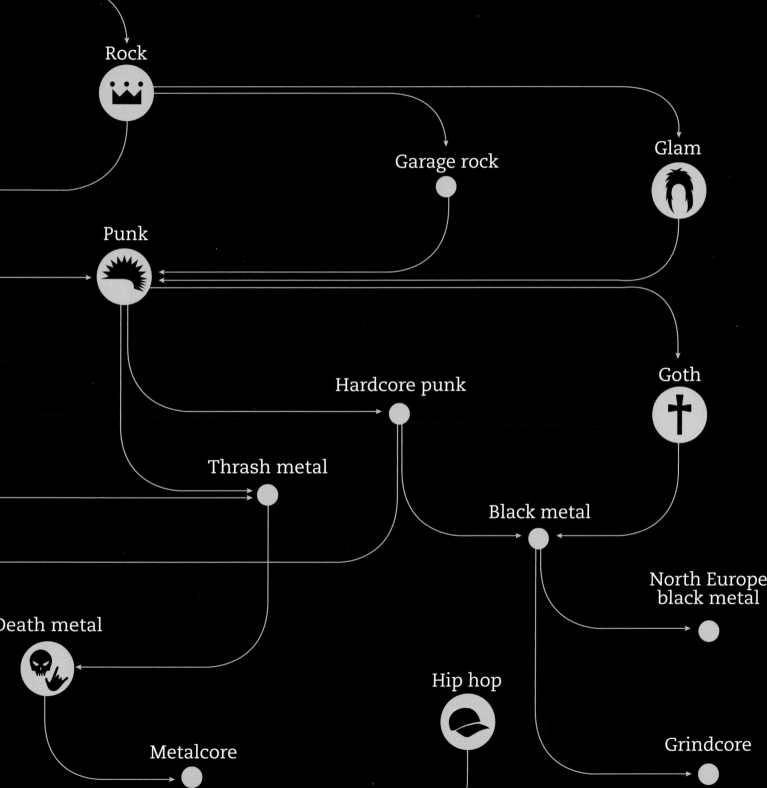

Rock

Garage rock

Glam

Punk

Hardcore punk

Goth

Thrash metal

Black metal

Death metal

North Europe
black metal

Hip hop

Metalcore

Grindcore

Deep Purple

Is one riff enough to enter the pantheon of rock music? Yes, it probably is, because the four notes of the riff in *Smoke on the Water* are more than enough for Deep Purple to earn a place there. Of course, encapsulating the long history of this English band in that riff alone, which has been imitated millions of times every day by millions of guitars throughout the world, would be unfair, since the story of Deep Purple is so rich and marked by so much success and truly great rock music.

First of all, it must be said that this band, together with Black Sabbath, Led Zeppelin and a few others, is one of the pioneers of hard rock. They have paved the way for various generations of musicians who, starting with the band's wise decision to break away from psychedelia by amplifying their instruments and emphasizing rhythm, have created a true genre. Yet Deep Purple is, again, much more than this. Over the years the band has had some extraordinary musicians who have extended the range of its production and creativity, passing from the symphonic rock of the initial phase to blues rock, and often flirting with the structures of progressive rock while always searching for new ideas and solutions. Albums such as *Deep Purple in Rock* offered the music of the early 1970s an approach that was different from the most sophisticated progressive rock with its intellectual overtones, reminding everyone that, whether you like or not, rock is and will always be a mixture of emotion and hard work, power and simplicity, sophistication and representation, egocentricity and spectacle, profundity and nonsense. This is the music of Deep Purple, characterized by absolutely overwhelming solos by guitarists like Ritchie Blackmore or Steve Morse, the incessant drumming of Ian Paice, the complex, intricate keyboard work of Jon Lord, the voice and shouting of Ian Gillan, and the musical gifts of the many others who were members of the English band at one point or another. All this resulted in an exceptional musical language that is at once popular, intelligible, immediate, entertaining and compelling in and of itself - never 'minimal' or essential, but always full of surprises and hints of genius.

Limiting Deep Purple's history to *Smoke on the Water* would be a mistake. Yet it can't be denied that its simple riff, plus the incredible fire that broke out during the Montreux Festival as Frank Zappa and his Mothers of Invention were performing, which inspired the composition of this song, Deep Purple demonstrated that rock can become unbelievably great by doing small things, like describing itself in a mere anecdote and encapsulating an emotion in just four notes. Quite an achievement, no doubt about it.

158   DEEP PURPLE, THE HISTORIC BRITISH HARD ROCK BAND FORMED IN THE LATE 1960S, IN A PHOTOGRAPH FROM 1980.

Deep Purple

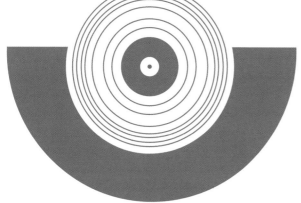

100

Millions of records sold.

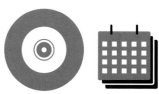

203

Number of weeks Deep Purple albums were among the Top 40 in the UK.

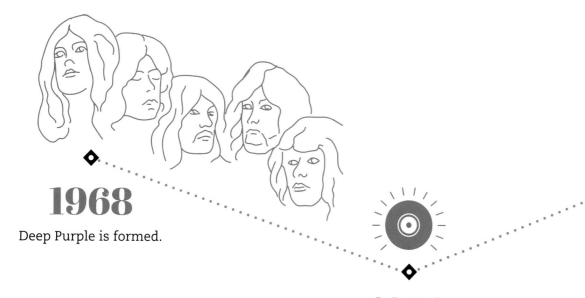

1968

Deep Purple is formed.

1970

Deep Purple in Rock is released.

1973

Ian Gillan leaves the band for the first time.

55

Total number of albums
(20 studio recordings and
35 recorded live).

44

Deep Purple singles
released.

14

Musicians who have been
in the band's lineup.

3

Deep Purple albums that
have topped the English
charts.

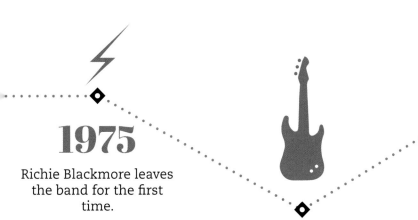

1975

Richie Blackmore leaves
the band for the first
time.

1994

Steve Morse joins the
band.

2012

John Lord dies.

2017

The year of what may be
the band's last tour.

Led Zeppelin

Almost forty years have passed since that December in 1980 when Led Zeppelin decided to break up. Yet, as in very few other cases in the history of rock (e.g. the Beatles), the public refused to admit that the group had disbanded and kept on buying their records, thus ensuring that the legend of one of the greatest English rock bands would continue on. In fact, it's rather strange to turn on the radio and still hear its music played every day throughout the world, as if Led Zeppelin were still active. Zeppelin's music has endured through time because it embodies rock in its most essential, direct form. Even if present-day rock has very little in common with the music that Led Zeppelin created, it is also true that whoever picks up an electric guitar must measure himself against what Jimmy Page, Robert Plant, John Paul Jones and John Bonham have achieved. Despite the fact that the band is often considered the founding father of heavy metal, Led Zeppelin really had little to do with that genre. The band absorbed various influences: various songs, a rich repertoire of acoustic guitar pieces, other songs influenced by Indian and Arabic music, pop, jazz - in other words, a myriad of various elements that helped create a sound that is truly unique. In any case, the starting point was always the blues. When the Yardbirds broke up in 1968, their bassist Jimmy Page decided to continue his music career with other musicians, and at the end of the year, he founded Led Zeppelin. He immediately understood that the blues was the ideal starting point for the realization of other genres, for music that was circulating and that involved thousands of young people in a world undergoing deep change. Page was (and is) certainly an incredible creator of guitar riffs. *Whole Lotta Love, Heartbreaker, Dazed and Confused, Black Dog, Immigrant Song*, and the highly famous *Moby Dick* demonstrate that most rock music of the 1970s and 1980s was based on his creativity, as hundreds of other guitarists simply drew from what Page had invented, adapting and recreating it. *Stairway to Heaven* is just one example, to this day one of the songs heard most on the radio the world over, containing most of the artful rock

162   THE MEMBERS OF LED ZEPPELIN IN 1968. FROM LEFT: JOHN PAUL JONES, ROBERT PLANT, JOHN BONHAM AND JIMMY PAGE.

163

of Led Zeppelin, its love for the blues, for music with
intense contrasts, songs that strike one for their sheer
energy as well as their tenderness and passion. The
Led Zeppelin experience is closely linked to the period
ranging from 1969, the year their first album was
released, to 1980, when the band broke up after the

death of John Bonham. A terrible loss for the other band
members, Bonham was not only a close friend but also the
heart of the group. Since then, the three remaining members
reunited a few times, and there was a fine but short-lived
Page and Plant collaboration. Through really, it doesn't
matter, because the Led Zeppelin airship is still soaring.

64 ROBERT PLANT ON STAGE AT EARL'S COURT WITH THE REST OF LED ZEPPELIN.

65 JOHN PAUL JONES, BASSIST, JIMMY PAGE, GUITARIST, JOHN BONHAM, PERCUSSION, AND ROBERT PLANT VOCALIST - THAT IS, LED ZEPPELIN - DURING A CONCERT

LED-ZEPPELIN

20

Number, in millions, of requests made for tickets for the concert of the one-time only Zeppelin reunion (with Jason Bonham, John's son, on drums), held on December 10, 2007 at the O2 Arena, London.

21,000

Number of tickets available for the O2 Arena concert. They were sold through an advance sale via an online random draw.

7

Albums that hit no. 1 on the British charts.

17

The number of albums in the solo career of vocalist Robert Plant (two together with Page), by far the most prolific, post-Zeppelin.

1968

The band is formed from the ashes of the disbanded Yardbirds.

1980

John Bonham dies and the band breaks up.

40

Shots of vodka that led to the death of John Bonham.

9

Albums produced by the band with its original lineup, plus four live recordings and nine compilations.

5

Band reunions for single events after the group broke up.

4

Albums with the same title, that is, the name of the band followed by Roman numerals respecting the chronological order of the releases (*Led Zeppelin I, II, III and IV*).

1

The Guinness record held by Led Zeppelin, awarded in 2008 for the Highest Demand for Tickets for One Music Concert.

0

Words on the cover of the album *Led Zeppelin IV*, which has the famous painting *The Hermit* and no title.

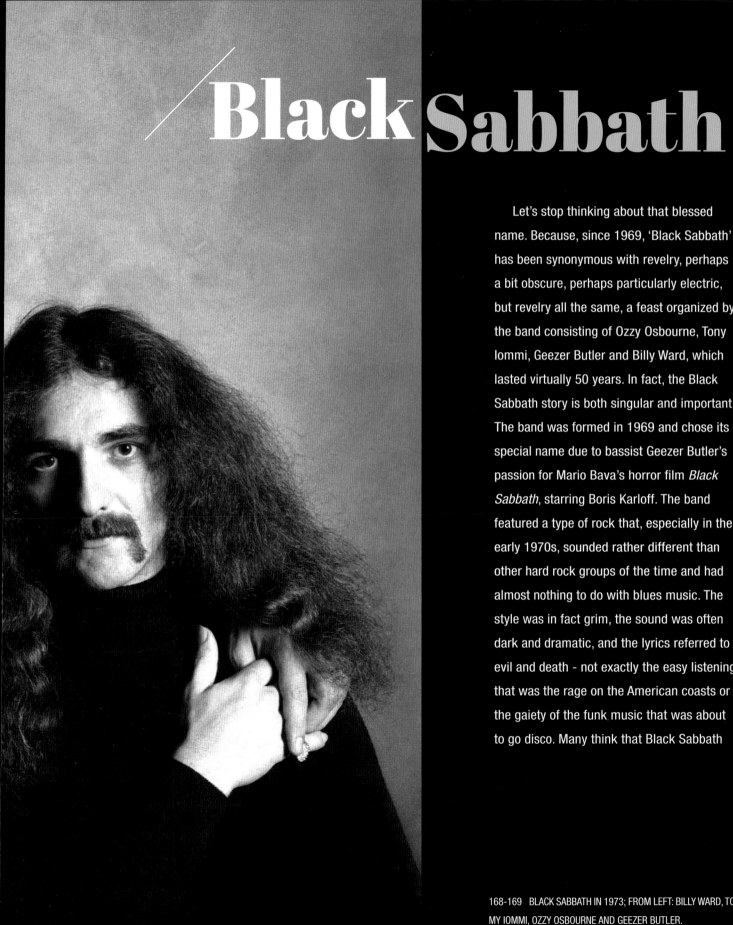

Black Sabbath

Let's stop thinking about that blessed name. Because, since 1969, 'Black Sabbath' has been synonymous with revelry, perhaps a bit obscure, perhaps particularly electric, but revelry all the same, a feast organized by the band consisting of Ozzy Osbourne, Tony Iommi, Geezer Butler and Billy Ward, which lasted virtually 50 years. In fact, the Black Sabbath story is both singular and important. The band was formed in 1969 and chose its special name due to bassist Geezer Butler's passion for Mario Bava's horror film *Black Sabbath*, starring Boris Karloff. The band featured a type of rock that, especially in the early 1970s, sounded rather different than other hard rock groups of the time and had almost nothing to do with blues music. The style was in fact grim, the sound was often dark and dramatic, and the lyrics referred to evil and death - not exactly the easy listening that was the rage on the American coasts or the gaiety of the funk music that was about to go disco. Many think that Black Sabbath

was the 'father' of heavy metal, but it must be said that many of the bands that became its 'successors' (some of them becoming very successful in the process), were not able to reproduce Sabbath's explosive innovation from the early 1970s. With albums such as *Paranoid, Sabbath Bloody Sabbath* and *Masters of Reality*, they laid down a style that they then helped to develop over the years. Anything but 'monolithic', Sabbath traversed 50 years of rock in a rather chaotic fashion, changing the lineup quite often, while always maintaining the nucleus of the four founding figures up to the end. Besides Ozzy, they had versatile and skilled vocalists such as Ronnie James Dio and, for a short period, even Ian Gillan. But in the collective imagination, Osbourne remained the sole Prince of Darkness, the one who deserved the role of band frontman. While Iommi's guitar, Butler's bass and Ward's drums most certainly helped create the band's powerful, dark sound, it was Osbourne's stage presence and voice that truly characterized the band, at the outset as well as in the many reunions and up to the final stages of the band's existence. He was an extravagant rock star with a history of legendary excesses, eventually even becoming the star of a reality show about him and his family (*The Osbournes*, which enjoyed four highly successful seasons on MTV), the creator of acts that lie between reality and myth (such as having bitten the head off a bat while on stage), and a singer with unmistakable style. Without him, Black Sabbath would have been a good rock band. With him, it became legendary.

70

Black Sabbath records sold, in millions.

75,000

Amount, in dollars, that the band spent on cocaine, according to Geezer Butler, during the recording of *Vol. 4*.

12

Hours the band spent recording its debut album.

7

Number of songs on the album.

10

Number of albums in the British Top Ten.

2

Sabbath albums that topped the charts.

1963 🎬

The year the film *Black Sabbath*, with Boris Karloff, was released.

1969

The band makes its debut as Black Sabbath.

1982

The year when, on January 20, Ozzy Osbourne bit off the head of a bat on stage, believing it was a toy made of rubber.

1989

Brian May of Queen plays on Sabbath's *When Death Calls*.

2002

Ozzy Osbourne becomes the star of the MTV reality show *The Osbournes*.

/AC/DC

It's the sound. Not just any sound, but the one produced by a band that is recognizable after just two seconds: the sound of AC/DC, which is to say the sound of hard rock. However, the 'hard rock' label certainly doesn't give us a clue as to what AC/DC really sounds like live. It isn't a question of quality; the band's bravura, power, constant enthusiasm and ability to entertain are indisputable. It's a question of quantity. As long ago as the 1980s, the band members would place two huge walls with 54 amplifiers on each side of the stage, a total of 70,000 watts – enough sound to shake a mountain. Nowadays they go even further, with only a few carefully gaged and well chosen elements: songs that are based on two or three chords, always high-pitched and raw, supported by a beat that even in the most relaxed moments is highly charged, plus simple and unforgettable riffs, catchy refrains that are easy to learn by heart.

In the words of guitarist Angus Young: "I'm sick and tired of people saying that we put out 13 albums that sound exactly the same. In fact, we've put out 14 albums that sound exactly the same." When performing live, the band's frontman runs from one end to the other of the enormous stages used by AC/DC, flopping on the floor, jumping and sweating like hell, while his guitar sends the audience into ecstasy. In fact, people go to AC/DC concerts to see him, and every sound he makes on that guitar is accompanied by their shouts, going crazy every time he plays a solo.

172-173 AC/DC IN FRONT OF THE SHEPPERTON FILM STUDIOS, LONDON (1976).

Young and his fellow bandsmen, who have all been replaced time and again over the years, have devoted their lives to the cause, never betraying it. And they have no intention of doing so: "And why should I?" Young said with a laugh, adding that all too often people have said that rock was dead. In th 1970s, one recording industry exec even told the band that they could stop their tours, that the guitar sound was finished, and from that time on the only real sound would be keyboard-based and progressive. "Well, keyboards and progressive have passed by and we're still here."

The story of AC/DC began with brothers Malcolm and Angus Young, who left Australia to conquer the music industry with their guitars, flanked by Bon Scott, their original, legendary vocalist who died many years ago, and by Brian Johnson, who replaced Scott and proved to be a great asset to the band. Due to health problems, Johnson himself was replaced by Axl Rose, their present vocalist. Many other band members have come and gone – bass guitarists, drummers and keyboard players – up to the recent death of Malcolm. Their repertory has many classic songs, from *Highway to Hell* to *It's a Long Way to the Top (If You Wanna Rock'n'roll)*, and from *Hell's Bells* to *Back in Black*, and over the years their style has become more restrained and polished and their shows more complete and complex. Yet Angus Young has not changed much and still appears dressed in his schoolboy 'uniform' holding his guitar: "I've got a lot of guitars but I only play one, always the same one; I've never changed it. And to be sure not to lose it I always put it under my bed in my bedroom. When I got married my wife asked me where I would put the guitar, and I answered, Under the bed, of course.' And it's still there."

74 AC/DC AGAIN IN 1976. ABOVE IS VOCALIST BON SCOTT, WHILE GUITARIST ANGUS YOUNG IS IN THE MIDDLE STICKING OUT HIS TONGUE.

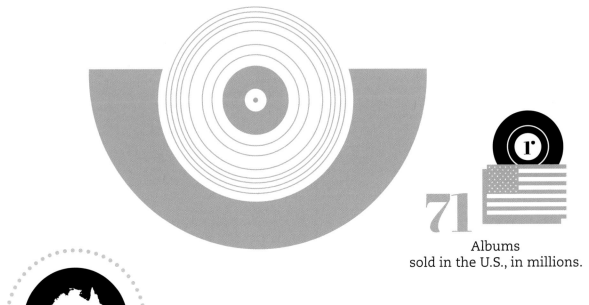

71

Albums
sold in the U.S., in millions.

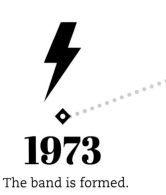

401

Concerts the band
has played in Australia.

34

Number
of countries in which
they have performed live.

26

The musicians that have
played in the band
in various roles.

1973

The band is formed.

1976

AC/DC signs a
contract with
Atlantic.

1979

Highway to Hell
is released.

1980

The band's
frontman,
Bon Scott, dies.

1,267

The number of times
the band has played
Back in Black live.

1

The only musician
who has always been
in the band: Angus Young.

AC/DC

Rolling Stone

2003

AC/DC is inducted to the Rock
and Roll Hall of Fame.

2008

The year the band
finally appeared on the
cover
of *Rolling Stone*.

2013

The band celebrates its 40th
anniversary.

2016

Axl Rose becomes
the AC/DC frontman.

Guns N' Roses

The year was 1985, and rock in America was not in the best of health. Some people thought that sheer boredom had buried rock 'n' roll for good, and they tried to give it one final shove before its demise, overwhelmed by new wave and hip hop. But instead, that 'shove' was provided by Guns N' Roses, and it was like an electric shock, a shock of 28 million copies sold of its debut album, *Appetite for Destruction*.

GNR was formed in Los Angeles from the ashes of two other groups, the L.A. Guns and Hollywood Rose, combining the two into a new name. The new group immediately became popular among the 'orphans' of rock, enjoying great success and an amazing career by offering "rock as it should be," consisting of all the possible clichés of this genre, recast to perfection. The band found an empty niche and quickly occupied it by attracting attention in every possible way. It soon rose on the charts, breaking all the rules of the game and often gaining more publicity than it deserved for reasons that were decidedly not related to music. Of the sex, drugs and rock 'n' roll trifecta, Guns N' Roses concentrated more on the second, and in fact its members' addiction problems led them to waste a good deal of their creative potential. The instability and unruliness of some of them did the rest. Yet despite the partying, transgressions, arguments and brawls among its members and with other musicians, Guns N' Roses was undeniably one of the most popular rock bands in the period bridging the 1980s and 1990s. Today it's even considered classic, attracting huge audiences at every concert. Naturally, not everybody likes the band. Singer

and songwriter John Lydon, someone who knows quite a lot about transgressive rock, once stated that at most of the members are like roadies who have just climbed on stage and are trying out their instruments. Certainly this is a rather reductive comment on one of the most explosive phenomena in contemporary rock, but Guns N' Roses, like an iron fist in a velvet glove, has never pretended to anything but what it really is. In other words, seeking original musical refinement has never been one of its priorities. Hard rock and metal are certainly not the only genres in the repertoire, which also includes power ballads, reinterpreted classic rock, and even some hints of pop. But the main objective would seem to be to enjoyment at all costs. Axl Rose has always been the band's driving force, even in its darkest moments. And still by his side in the latest, umpteenth rebirth of the band, are Slash and Duff McKagan, forming the perfect trio of 'renegades' who, disregarding fashions, electronic rock, hip hop and dance music, and refusing to acknowledge the various musical trends that have appeared over the last forty years, continue to believe that rock must consist mostly of energy, noise and fun. And if you don't like it, then look somewhere else.

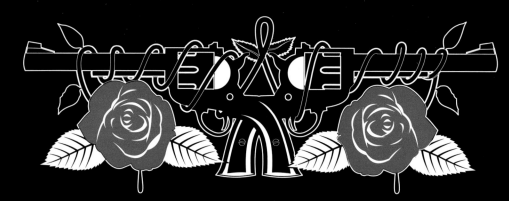

Guns N' Roses

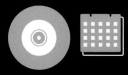

14

Years it took
to produce
their latest album,
Chinese Democracy.

13

Dollars, in millions,
the same album cost
the producer, once again
the singer Axl Rose.

1509

The year Raphael
painted *The School of
Athens*, the famous
fresco a detail of
which is on the covers
of both *Use Your Illusion*
albums.

1985

The 5-man band led
by singer Axl Rose
and guitarist Slash
is formed.

1992

An altercation breaks
out at the MTV Video
Music Awards between
Axl Rose and Kurt
Cobain, with the latter
accusing Rose of
trying to sleep with his
fiancée, Courtney Love.

100

Millions of records the band has sold worldwide, with only six studio records produced to date.

28

Copies sold, in millions, of their debut album, *Appetite for Destruction* (1987).

23

Number of musicians who alternated - in the studio and live - in the band's 15 lineups to date.

4

Dollars, in millions, Axl Rose spent to rent the oil tanker he jumped from in the *Estranged* video.

10

Runtime in minutes (plus 13 seconds) of *Coma,* their longest song.

2

Spectators who attended the first Guns N' Roses concert in Los Angeles.

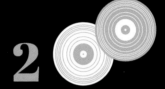

2

Albums (vinyl version) of their major work, *Use Your Illusion I and II* released a few days after one another in September 1991.

2006

Axl Rose is arrested during a Stockholm concert for having bitten a security guard on the leg.

2012

Guns N' Roses is inducted to the Rock and Roll Hall of Fame.

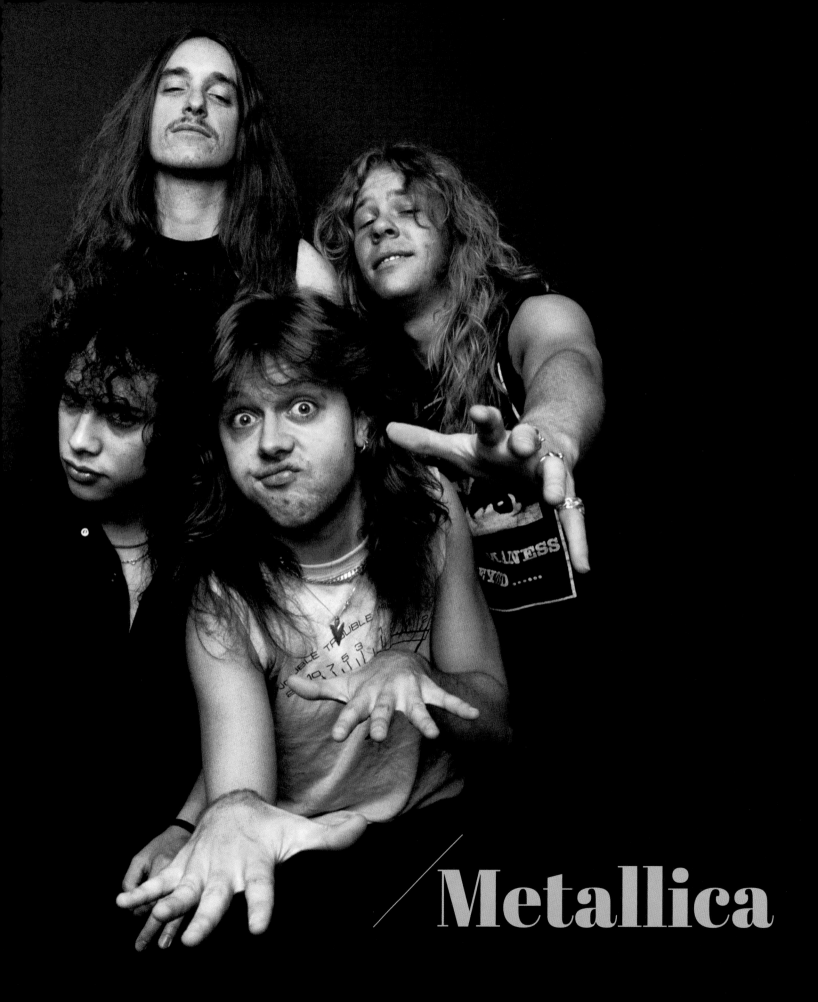

Metallica

With such a name it's not difficult to understand what the band's music is like: 'heavy metal' in the total sense of the word. Durable, compact, hard and ultra-powerful music that takes your breath away, that hits you like a wave and leaves you in a daze. Metallica aficionados consider their first four albums masterpieces, records that established the style of a group that is aggressive but also able to communicate with a broader public. Unlike most metal bands, Metallica has managed to conquer a great many fans who were quite distant from the metal world. In the 1990s, it even entered the 'mainstream' without betraying its metal roots and original musical objective. *Enter Sandman* and the ballad *Nothing Else Matters* are prime examples.

Hailing from California, Metallica has passed through several lineup changes, but it has always revolved around James Hetfield, Lars Ulrich and Kirk Hammet, a perfect trio seeking a difficult balance between excess and normality, heavy metal and emotion. This is by no means a monolithic metal band; Metallica doesn't seek success simply by repeating itself. Its members have always taken and experimented with new, divergent paths, often missing the target but always demonstrating to critics of this musical genre that metal is not the obsessive repetition of a pattern. Convincing proof of this is the work that has been most criticized and discussed: the band's singular collaboration with rock singer and songwriter Lou Reed to produce the album *Lulu*, which, above and beyond the final result, showed without a doubt that Metallica wanted to go well beyond everything is predictable and taken for granted. A career of almost 40 years has transformed the band into the very emblem of metal in the minds of the public at large. Its members, for their part, have personified this concept with conviction and honesty, well aware they are on a risky expressive tightrope, so to speak, where it is easier to make a mistake than get it right. But the incredible talent of the 'four horsemen', especially when performing live, is still nothing short of unique.

182 METALLICA, THE MOST SUCCESSFUL CALIFORNIA METAL BAND IN THE 1990S. CLOCKWISE FROM ABOVE: CLIFF BURTON, JAMES HETFIELD, KIRK HAMMET AND LARS ULRICH.

183 METALLICA ON STAGE AT THE ASIA/WORLD EXPO IN HONG KONG ON JANUARY 20, 2017

METALLICA

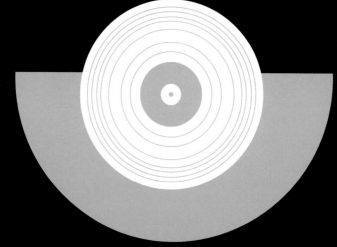

125

Records sold to date, in millions, including 60 million in the United States alone.

1981

James Hetfield, Lars Ulrich, Kirk Hammett and Cliff Burton form Metallica in Los Angeles.

1983

Dave Mustaine is ejected (going on to found Megadeth) and replaced by Kirk Hammett. The band releases its debut album, *Kill 'Em All*, the 'father' of thrash metal.

1984

The *Call of Ktulu* (from the album *Ride the Lightning*) is the band's tribute to the horror atmosphere created by H.P. Lovecraft. In 2001 the song won the band's sixth Grammy for the Best Rock Instrumental Performance with the symphonic version played by the San Francisco Symphony under Michael Kamen.

1986

Master of Puppets (the single from the album of the same name, considered their masterpiece) reaches third place in the VH1 ranking of the 40 Greatest Metal Songs Ever.

11

To date, the total number of Metallica studio albums. But their discography also includes four live albums, one compilation, one soundtrack, five EPs and over 40 singles.

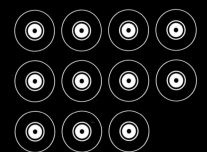

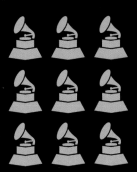

9

Grammy Awards won by the 4-member band.

2000

The band files a lawsuit against Napster Inc. and its peer-to-peer file-sharing to defend artists' performing rights.

Bassist Cliff Burton dies in an accident on the bus the band was using during a tour in Europe. The musicians drew cards to see who would choose what bunk to sleep in. Burton won and chose Kirk Hammett's bunk.

2011

The year of the release of *Lulu*, a collaboration concept album that draws inspiration from Wedekind's plays. On it, Metallica accompanies Lou Reed. This was the New York singer-songwriter's last album.

2013

The year of Metallica's concert film, *Through the Never*, which alternates footage of the band performing with a fantasy thriller plot.

Progressive

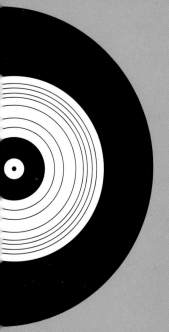

In the four years from 1969 to 1973, rock not only revolutionized Western music, but also rose to the status of the highest and most complex expressive procedure of the 20th century. This is no exaggeration. In that brief period, rock with the generic and fascinating label 'progressive' had the exceptional aim of describing life and dreams, imagining the future and re-interpreting the past, establishing new rules without losing sight of the roots by also offering a definition of contemporaneity. Progressive rock was a unique phenomenon, with a limited time span, explosively creative and decidedly not a genre, strictly speaking. In short, there was not only one meaning of 'progressive', but dozens, hundreds, even thousands, depending on how many bands were placed under its umbrella. For example, there was the entire sector of bands that harked back to popular traditions; those that approached avant-garde electronica; and another one closely connected to rock; bands that drew inspiration from classical music or were strongly influenced by jazz or contemporary music; and there were always simple songs, while many other bands based their performances on theater. Yes, 'progressive' was an ocean. It was the subgenre of rock that had gained its absolute, total freedom, capable of moving through styles, genres, eras and sounds in a markedly creative

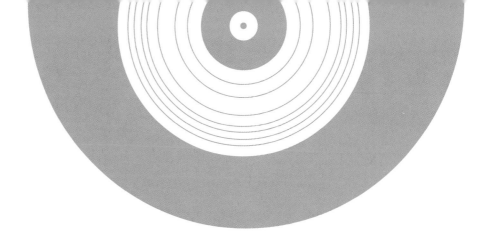

manner. And, it was distinctly European. The English roots were there for all to see. There is no denying that King Crimson, Genesis and Yes were the 'triad' of Progressive, but it is equally true that freedom of expression and the possibility of being inspired by different cultures and sounds led to the formation of progressive rock bands throughout Europe (Italy, France, Spain, Germany and northern Europe), bands that not only could compete on equal terms with their English counterparts, but above all were supported by their close relationship with the public in their respective countries. So, this was 'high' music, most of which was written down somewhere, but which the musicians played by heart, music with many references to literature and with sophisticated, highly elaborate lyrics. It was music often constructed in the form of suites or was complex, music which the public listened to while seated, extremely attentive and silent, unlike audience behavior up to a few years earlier.

From 1969 to 1973, progressive music imagined the unimaginable and rock moved freely in every possible direction, merging various styles. Then grandiloquence, commercialization, the creation of ever more elaborate spectacles, the lifestyle of musicians who by now had become rock stars, the lack of that electric yet peaceful chaos that had been part of every concert - all led 'prog' to become cold and distant, technically more and more perfect yet sterile and meaningless. Up to the rise of punk, which put all these bands out to pasture.

Progressive

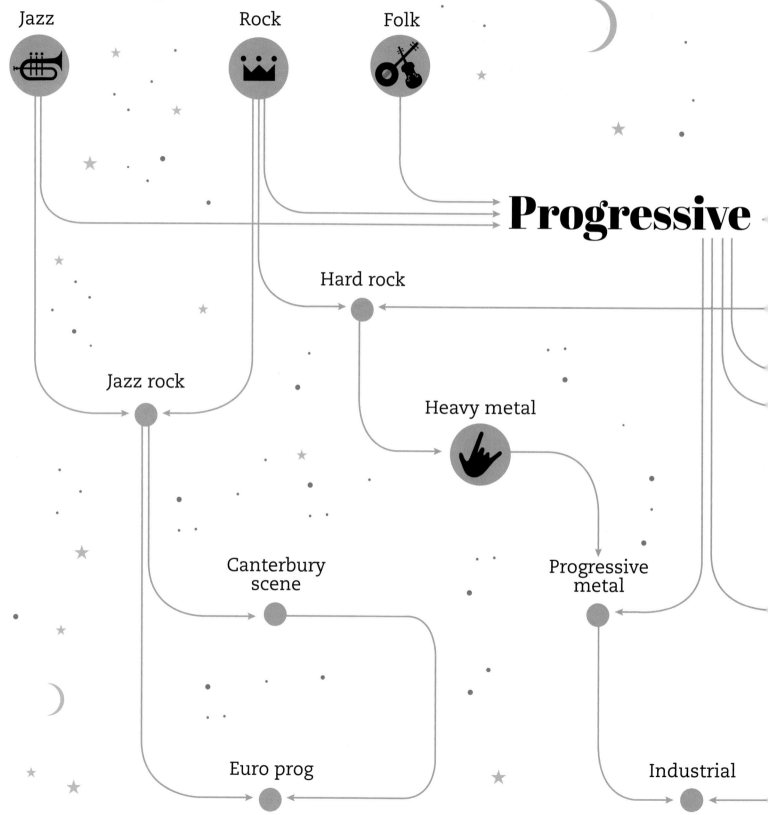

Jazz

Rock

Folk

Progressive

Hard rock

Jazz rock

Heavy metal

Canterbury scene

Progressive metal

Euro prog

Industrial

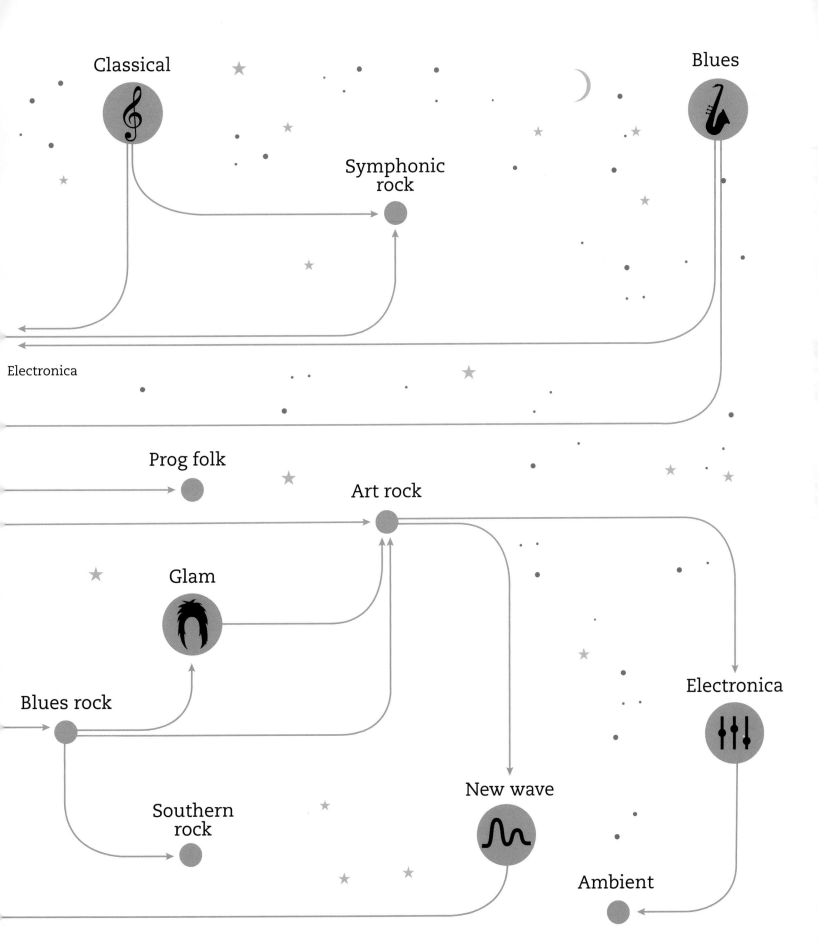

Classical

Symphonic rock

Blues

Electronica

Prog folk

Art rock

Glam

Electronica

Blues rock

New wave

Southern rock

Ambient

Frank Zappa

A genius. There is no better word to describe Frank Zappa: a musician, composer, orchestra conductor, exceptional creator, one of the greatest musicians of the 20th century, one of the few able to work with various genres, styles and sounds to make them his very own. There was no 'high' or 'low' music in Zappa's eclectic universe, no separation between classical and rock; there was only the joy of creation, composition, improvisation, as well as of provocation and mockery. A determined non-conformist born in Baltimore on December 21, 1940, Francis Vincent Zappa began to play drums and guitar when he attended Antelope Valley High School. In 1964, he formed a band called the Muthers, later changing it to the Mothers and then, in 1966, after the band had signed its first recording contract with Verve, he changed it once again to the Mothers of Invention (referring ironically to both Mother's Day and the famous proverb "Necessity is the mother of invention"). With the new name, Zappa released his debut album in June that same year, *Freak Out*, a true manifesto of the creative musicality of an artist that reveals what he and his group offered during their concerts in that period, including happenings and extremely provocative lyrics. After the release of his second album, *Absolutely Free* (extensively censored by record company executives because of the 'scandalous' themes in the lyrics, including remixing certain 'forbidden' words to make them unintelligible), Zappa created a ferocious satire of the hippie psychedelia of that period, and especially of the Beatles, with his third album *We're Only in It for the Money*, the cover of which is mockingly similar to the cover of the English quartet's *Sgt. Pepper*. Zappa rejected all trends and labels, and despite himself was considered the king of American counterculture because of his performances, albums, and even certain posters (the most famous of which has photographs of him sitting on the toilet in his apartment). In 1968 he severed his contract with Verve. This marked the beginning of a war against 'official' record companies that lasted many years and that led Zappa to work with two labels he managed for Warner Bros., Bizarre and Straight, and then, many years later, to found Zappa Records and lastly his own recording company, Barking Pumpkin. The Mothers of Invention continued its multiform activity until 1970, when Zappa decided to break up the band since he was "tired of the public that always applauds at the wrong moment." The band's last concert was held in May that same year, at the UCLA Pavilion with the Los Angeles Philharmonic Orchestra directed by Zubin Metha. Zappa's 'new course' in the 1970s was not received with enthusiasm by the public and critics, although it was a prolific feat (six albums in three years). The records enjoyed a limited success and the concerts didn't fare much better, up to the disastrous European tour in 1971, when the band lost all its equipment after a fire broke out in the Casino of Montreux (inspiring Deep Purple's famous song *Smoke on the Water*). This ill-fated year ended with another disaster, when one of the spectators at a London concert pushed Zappa off the stage, causing serious injuries.

190   A 1979 PORTRAIT OF FRANK ZAPPA WEARING AN UNCLE SAM HAT.

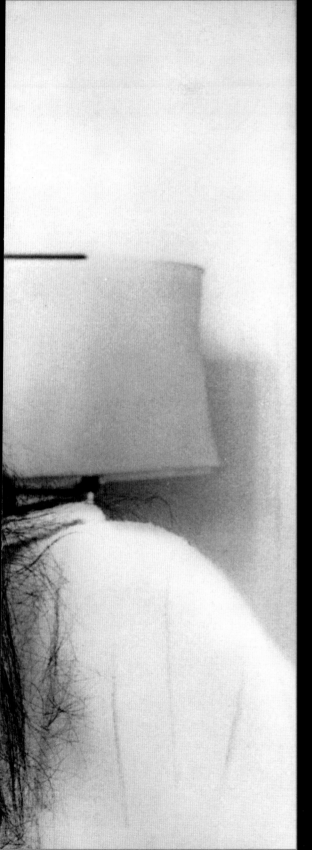

The 1970s and 1980s witnessed numerous examples of his eclectic style. The many albums he released contain rock parodies, subversive exuberance, atonal music, jokes and double entendres, monumental works for guitar, musical theater, and ever-changing concerts - all overflowing with that extraordinary, captivating inventiveness that has always characterized his oeuvre. After receiving the Legion of Honor Award in France from Minister of Culture Jack Lang, in 1990 Zappa was invited to Czechoslovakia by President Vaclav, a great admirer of his, who offered the musician a post as cultural ambassador, which the American State Department vigorously opposed. It was impossible to pigeonhole Zappa; restrictive labels just didn't stick He often took a polemical stance against the world of rock, and his satire 'offended' more or less everyone over the years. But he also fought a long battle against censorship, in particular against the Parents Music Resource Center, the association headed by the wife of US Vice President Al Gore, Tipper Gore. In 1991, Zappa even decided to become an independent candidate in the American presidential election: "Could I do any worse than Ronald Reagan?" was his slogan. Yet, the election campaign never took off: in November 1991 he was invited to participate in a concert that would be a tribute to him, titled *Zappa' s Universe*, but he didn't show up. His oldest sons, Moon Unit and Dweezil (Zappa had two other children, Ahmet and Diva), explained his absence by announcing his illness. Zappa's last live appearance was with the Ensemble Modern, at Frankfurt, when they played *The Yellow Shark*, in September 1992, shortly before he died. Zappa left a huge void in the music world, which, without him has sadly become a bit more normal.

Frank Zappa

111

Number of official Zappa albums to date.

62

Albums released by the musician during his 27-year career.

49

Albums released posthumously by the Zappa Family Trust.

1966

The year *Freak Out* was released, the debut album of one of the most monumental discographies in the history of rock.

1965

The Mothers of Invention is formed.

1971

The year when, at Montreux, toward the end of a concert by Frank Zappa and the Mothers of Invention, a spectator shot a flare that triggered the fire that destroyed the entire Casino, a disaster narrated in Deep Purple's world-famous *Smoke on the Water.*

1972

Zappa appears as a sideman on the album *Some Time in New York City*, by John Lennon and Yoko Ono/Plastic Ono Band.

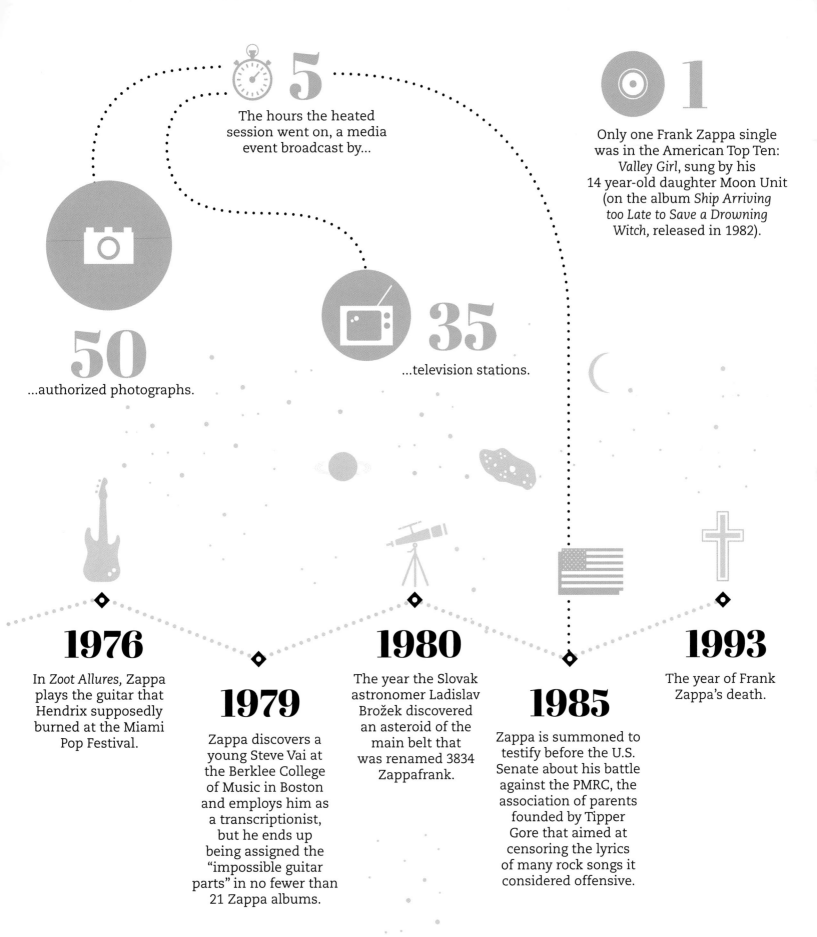

5

The hours the heated session went on, a media event broadcast by...

1

Only one Frank Zappa single was in the American Top Ten: *Valley Girl*, sung by his 14 year-old daughter Moon Unit (on the album *Ship Arriving too Late to Save a Drowning Witch*, released in 1982).

50

...authorized photographs.

35

...television stations.

1976

In *Zoot Allures*, Zappa plays the guitar that Hendrix supposedly burned at the Miami Pop Festival.

1979

Zappa discovers a young Steve Vai at the Berklee College of Music in Boston and employs him as a transcriptionist, but he ends up being assigned the "impossible guitar parts" in no fewer than 21 Zappa albums.

1980

The year the Slovak astronomer Ladislav Brožek discovered an asteroid of the main belt that was renamed 3834 Zappafrank.

1985

Zappa is summoned to testify before the U.S. Senate about his battle against the PMRC, the association of parents founded by Tipper Gore that aimed at censoring the lyrics of many rock songs it considered offensive.

1993

The year of Frank Zappa's death.

It really doesn't matter whether or not you like progressive rock: Genesis was one of the fundamental bands for the development of rock in the 1970s and a hugely successful pop band in the 1980s and 1990s. In fact, it was really two different bands. There is the one that, at the dawn of the 1970s, created totally innovative new music that was a remarkably intelligent mixture of rock, classical, folk, theater, avant-garde and pop. These songs were not written, but required a great deal of attention and skill. They were more like suites than songs, music that drew fully from other genres and integrated them perfectly. The second band was the one formed after the separate departures of Peter Gabriel and Steve Hackett. When Phil Collins became the frontman, Genesis was transformed into an almost ideal 'pop machine' that could put new electronic music and soul on the same wavelength, producing highly popular songs which in some cases were even suitable as dance music.

Obviously, the Genesis legend is related to the first phase of the band's career, ranging from 1969 to 1974: five amazing years during which the band released six albums, five of them historic due to an innovative rock style, which was taken where it had never been before. In 1970, when the band released its second album, *Trespass*, it began a creative process that overwhelmed everything

and everyone: greatly stretching the boundaries of what would be called progressive rock, combining improvisation and written parts, going beyond the canonical norms of songwriting, and making major breakthroughs by merging genres and styles. The band revolved around Peter Gabriel, with his voice and highly original stage presence. In the wake of what David Bowie had begun to do a short time earlier, Gabriel brought theatricality into the rock scene by means of ever-changing 'costumes' and personas, thus making the visual element an essential feature of a project that, when performed live, became much different from the albums recorded in the studio.

When in 1975, after the release of the band's most ambitious project, *The Lamb Lies Down on Broadway*, and its long related tour, Gabriel decided to leave Genesis, many people thought the band was coming to an end. This seemed to be confirmed, after the release of a double album, by Steve Hackett's departure in 1977 and the explosion of punk. But with Phil Collins as their frontman, Genesis went through a metamorphosis and responded to the punk revolution by abandoning their old style and becoming a new band: less over the top and innovative, less surprising, but rather pop-oriented and a great success, without any nostalgia for the past. Two stories, two lives, and so much music that is still with us.

Genesis

500,000

Number of spectators at the band's last European concert, held at the Circus Maximus in Rome.

140

The number, in millions, of the records sold globally.

1967

The year Genesis was formed.

1972

Peter Gabriel begins to wear various costumes during live performances to interpret the 'characters' in the songs.

1973

The album *Selling England by the Pound* is released and includes the band's first popular single, *I Know What I Like.*

1975

Peter Gabriel leaves the band.

15

Studio albums that Genesis produced.

7

Musicians who have collaborated with the band.

11

The members of the band over the years.

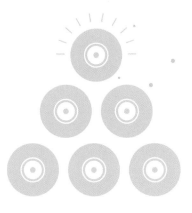

6

Platinum albums awarded to Genesis.

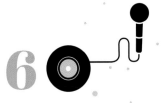

6

The live albums.

2

The two persons who were always in the band's lineup: Tony Banks and Mike Rutherford.

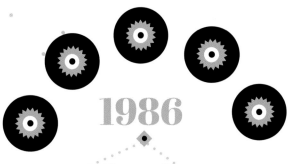

1986

The year five Genesis singles made it to the top ten.

2007

The band breaks up.

1977

Steve Hackett also leaves the band.

1996

Phil Collins leaves the band.

Alternative & Indie

There was once a time when rock was just rock, and that was that. It didn't matter much if it contained elements of the Latin rhythms of Carlos Santana, the blues of the Rolling Stones, or the Grateful Dead's psychedelia. It was rock and that was enough. Then the public became fragmented into different tribes and families, and rock music followed youth culture as it developed, acquiring a myriad of different names and subgenres – with one exception: 'alternative' or 'indie' rock. The two terms are often superimposable, albeit not completely, and rather than a specific genre or sound, they indicate an approach to the music industry.

Come to think of it, it's odd, since the names of music genres normally derive from a rhythm, sound or style, and certainly not from a market category. But in this case, it is precisely being 'alternative' to or 'independent' from the wealthy and complex system of major record labels that characterizes the part of rock music that began and developed from the late 1980s onwards, arising from new wave and post punk. Therefore, the alternative music universe now includes bands that have enjoyed plenty of success and signed contracts with major labels after becoming well known. As a result, they have managed to retain a large measure of independence regarding their artistic choices. But it also includes small and very small bands that have continued to play the club circuit, be broadcast on college radio stations, keeping a particularly vivacious musical scene alive at a time when the record industry seemed to be controlling everything and everyone. Being 'independent' and 'alternative' meant, among other things, founding and developing free-spirited, creative record labels from one side of the Atlantic to the other; it meant dozens and dozens of different musical 'styles', from that of Sonic Youth to R.E.M., to give a clear example.

But it wasn't just a question of rock. More precisely, it was about the many forms taken by youth culture, especially in the 1990s, after the explosion of grunge, and in the 2000s, when 'indie' and 'alternative' also meant success, in both England and the U.S. There are indie singer-songwriters, pop indie bands, alternative folk bands and even country bands, which goes to show that the terms are more generational than strictly musical.

Those who shun consumer music, tend to like indie and alternative music, preferring to be part of a world where everything is still possible, where topping the charts is not obligatory and becoming famous is a mere accident. Today, after the digital revolution and the rise of streaming, and at a time when the major labels that truly dominate the market are lacking, the definitions of 'alternative' and 'indie' have less meaning, even though they still are alive and kicking.

Alternative & Indie

Garage rock

Hard rock

Glam

Punk

Goth

Post punk

Grunge

Indie rock

Emo

Post rock

Shoegaze

Dreampop

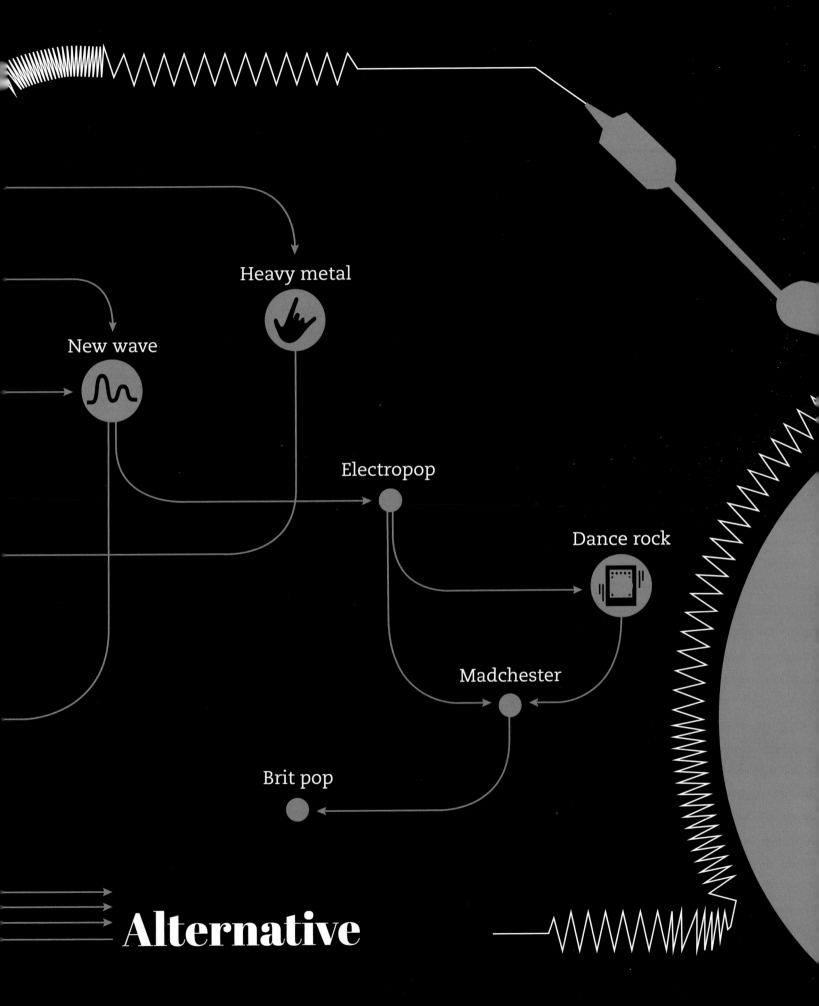

Heavy metal

New wave

Electropop

Dance rock

Madchester

Brit pop

Alternative

The Cure

Music that's almost brooding, gloomy: the Cure creates and conceals fascinating sounds and styles between one album and another, made of dreams, nightmares, passions, rhythms and melodies that follow one another incessantly to create a captivating, unique whole. The Cure might be called the most original and personal band that emerged from the singular movement that has been broadly given the 'goth' label. In fact, The Cure gradually broke free from the necessarily schematic elements of whatever 'goth' might be in order to produce complete, full, original music containing just about every element of rock from the 1980s and 1990s: the innovative energy of new wave, the creativity of the English music scene, in constant movement, together with a commitment to renewal and rebirth that has ensures the band never repeats itself. The stage is occupied by Robert Smith's minimal, simple gestures and his 'goth' image, which is both extravagant and familiar. Smith is in fact the Cure, and the soul of the band's sound is hidden among the chords of his guitar (always played masterfully in with his unmistakable style) and in his voice, which stands out above the thick texture of the band's instrumentals. The Cure's music, whether on records or live, is truly incredible as far as rock is concerned. It is based on a highly modern sensitivity while at the same time calling to mind psychedelia and inner journeys connected to the past. It is sensual, dream-like music that stimulates the imagination;

its relationship with the audience is total emotional fusion. Smith does not preach, nor does he have a messianic aura. Along with the rest of the band, he eludes the rock iconography that would have its stars accept showmanship as an end in itself; he has a punk ethic, albeit filtered by a poetic imagination that achieves highly-dramatic results while also conveying unbelievable positive energy.

Emerging with new wave in the 1980s and becoming true superstars the following decade, in the new millennium the Cure is still among us, having gone through many changes, phases, periods, and different seasons. Their music has become a classic, imitated by hundreds of other bands. It is adored by an expansive, faithful fan base that loves to explore the dark heart of a kind of rock that refuses to be pigeonholed, that eludes simplistic categorization, rock that can be filled with pain and lightness, with poetry and drama, and that after almost 40 years still sounds new and surprising.

204 THE CURE IN 1991. CLOCKWISE FROM ABOVE: BORIS WILLIAMS, SIMON GALLUP, ROGER O'DONNELL, ROBERT SMITH AND PORL (NOW PEARL) THOMPSON.

205 THE CURE AT ROSKILDE FESTIVAL IN 2013.

THE CURE

1956

Robert Smith, the undisputed leader of the Cure and dark icon of British new wave, is born.

1976

After Obeslisk, Malice and Easy Cure, the band becomes the Cure.

1978

Their first single, *Killing an Arab*, inspired by Albert Camus's novel *The Stranger*, is released. After the 9/11 terrorist attacks, it was banned by the American radio stations as anti-Islamic, and The Cure stopped playing it during concerts until the summer of 2005.

1980

The entire band is arrested by the Dutch police for taking a dip in the water on a beach where swimming is prohibited.

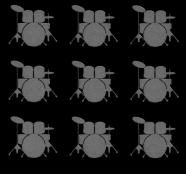

9

The changes in the lineup of the band, which has had four, three, and even briefly, two members.

3

Maximum duration of each of the band's various lineups in terms of studio albums produced.

1982

Pornography, considered the band's greatest album by its goth-est fans, is released.

1983

Robert Smith, who at the time was the guitarist of Siouxsie and the Banshees, insists on releasing a Beatles cover, *Dear Prudence*, which turned out to be their most successful hit, peaking at no. 3 on the British charts.

1992

Wish is the Cure's first no. 1 album on the English charts.

2011

Director Paolo Sorrentino used Robert Smith's stage look as inspiration for the protagonist of *This Must Be the Place*, played by Sean Penn.

Depeche Mode

When Depeche Mode stepped on stage in 1981, no one would have bet a nickel they'd become famous. In fact, reviews in music magazines vied with one another in lambasting the band. But Depeche Mode is still in fine fettle. In fact, it has gone from a teen band with improbable clothes to contemporary electronic music legends, from the merry dance beats of their beginnings to a dark, passionate group. Indeed, DM has always recognized and satisfied the tastes of the public by constantly evolving, touching upon grunge, Britpop, techno and trip hop, always playing a leading role in these 'movements' and, when all is said and done, without ever compromising its authenticity. Depeche Mode has been the most consistent and interesting interpreter of what was called electropop, which gradually became an original form of electronic, dark rock. However, DM's career has been anything but smooth sailing. Two major crises have shaped its fate: first, the decision on the part of such leading members as Vince Clarke and Alan Wilder to leave the band, and, perhaps more importantly, the self-destructive behavior of frontman Dave Gahan, who went from the merry 'pop' years in the early 1980s to a period of desperation, heroin addiction and poor health that led him to several brushes with death. His rebirth and return led to a 'second wind' for Depeche Mode, which, along with Martin Gore and Andrew Fletcher, miraculously rose from its ashes like a phoenix. Of the huge wave of synth-based bands, Depeche Mode is the only one that

has not only continued well into the new millennium with dignity, but has actually managed to increase its success without abandoning the sound that made it famous, honing a style that has become increasingly personal and convincing. *Music for the Masses*, one its most successful albums, is also a particularly apt definition of what this band creates, although, leaving aside its formulas, the music of Depeche Mode moves adroitly between dance-able pop atmospheres and songs that are closer to dark electronica with a sentimental, melodic feel. When performing live, the band is the epitome of professionalism, one of the best shows you could hope to see, a highly vivacious interplay of lights, revolving backdrops, laser effects and images that merge admirably with the music. For that matter, their live shows perfectly embody the band's ethos, committed first and foremost to the realm of images, releasing ingenious work in terms of video clips and photography.

208 DEPECHE MODE BACKSTAGE AT MADISON SQUARE GARDEN, NEW YORK IN 1987. FROM LEFT, ANDY FLETCHER, MARTIN GORE, DAVE GAHAN AND ALAN WILDER.

209 DAVE GAHAN ON STAGE AT THE LONDON O2 ARENA IN 2017.

Depeche Mode

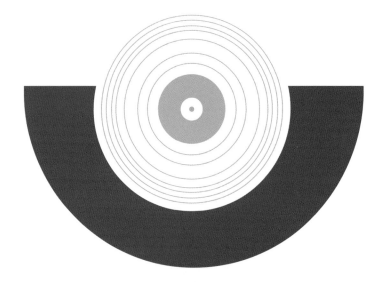

100

Records sold, in millions, by the British trio (formerly a quartet) thanks to its 14-album discography.

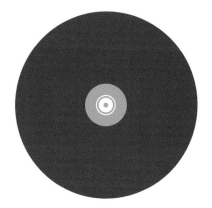

56

Singles released by the 'hurried fashion' band (the name was taken from a French fashion periodical, *Dépêche mode*).

1980

The year of the mythical English synth pop band. was formed

1989

The year of the guitar: *Personal Jesus* is the band's first single based on a four-chord riff instead of synth pop. It went gold in the U.S. and platinum in Italy.

17

Number of tours from 1980 to 2018.

3

Members in the current lineup: Dave Gahan (vocals), Martin L. Gore (guitar and keyboard), and Andrew Fletcher (keyboard, bass guitar and backing vocals). The number of former members and sidemen is 11.

11

Video clips produced for the band by the great photographer and director Anton Corbijn, who has been the author of many covers and photographs of Depeche Mode.

2

Minutes the paramedics had declared Gahan dead before managing to resuscitate him. After this experience, frontman Dave Gahan was determined to break free from his drug addiction.

2

Dave Gahan broke two ribs while stage diving during the band's Devotional Tour in 1993.

1996

Dave Gahan's heart stops due to an overdose of speedball (cocaine and heroin) giving the impression that he was dead.

2002

The year of country: Johnny Cash releases his last live album, *American IV: The Man Comes Around*, featuring a moving acoustic version of *Personal Jesus*.

Radiohead

Far removed from fashions, trends, and the rules that dictate the market, Radiohead is the only true manifestation of a musical soul that to some degree could still be called rock. And they prove it over and over again, with every new album. The first sensation you get when listening to a Radiohead record is sheer amazement. Nothing is as it should be; all the rules of musical communication are immediately overturned. Every song contains an entire world of sound that soon unfolds, completely enveloping and engaging the listener. This is not 'light music', there is no way you can let these songs roll off your back as if they were mere entertainment. The Oxford band draws only what is needed from present-day musical trends, discarding all that is superfluous, obvious and redundant. Though they often risk losing popularity, they end up actually enjoying greater success, because so many music fans out there recognize their authentic, solid alternative to prevailing musical consumerism, 'cute' bands planned and created by the record industry, especially prevalent in the 1990s when Thom Yorke and his fellow bandmates arrived on the scene. There is no doubt that Radiohead is rock. Not a genre but an attitude, not a sound but a manner of creating, a kind of freedom that merges different elements and cultures, and in which one encapsulates history and the stories the band considers important. There is nothing simple in Radiohead's music, nothing casual, no desire whatsoever to merely entertain. The band seeks to stimulate the listener's brain, it loves to be thought-provoking and, instead of making audiences dream, it tries to let them see reality through different eyes. However, this doesn't mean that their compositions are unlistenable avant-garde or that they do nothing to make their projects comprehensible to the greatest number of consumers possible. Radiohead's music has everything: melody, ballads, experimentation, celebration, enthusiasm and rhythm. The creative freedom of Radiohead is now total, absolute, though such freedom doesn't mean useless experimentation. Instead, it's a way to construct a perfect, ambitious project that traces the confines and contours of present-day rock while avoiding stereotypes. Then there's Yorke's fascinating voice, which can both upset and bewitch, be totally dominating and determine the qualities of a band that is quite at ease with various sounds, lying between the gelid rhythm of computers and a searing, relentless passion for communication. The members of Radiohead want to speak to the heart, not only to the brain, and they succeed – something that very few musicians in the new millennium have managed to do.

212 A 1994 PHOTOGRAPH OF RADIOHEAD. FROM LEFT: ED O'BRIEN, JOHNNY GREENWOOD, THOM YORKE, PHIL SELWAY AND COLIN GREENWOOD.

213 THOM YORKE AND JOHNNY GREENWOOD OF RADIOHEAD DURING A CONCERT HELD AT THE SYDNEY ENTERTAINMENT CENTER IN 2012.

Radiohead

Copies sold of *OK Computer*, in millions. Five of its twelve tracks were then released as singles.

30

Records sold, in millions, by the English four-man band, which has produced nine studio albums (plus a remix), one live album, four compilations and 30 singles.

1996

Radiohead produces *Exit Music (For a Film)*, a song written specially for the end credits of Baz Luhrmann's *William Shakespeare's Romeo + Juliet*. However, the track is not included on the soundtrack and is released in the band's following album, *OK Computer* (1997).

1985

On a Friday, the future Radiohead, is formed.

8

Years that passed before the release of *Pablo Honey*, the band's debut album.

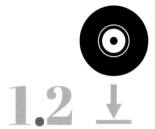

1.2 ↓

Album downloads, in millions, on the day *In Rainbows* was released.

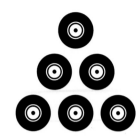

6

Radiohead albums that topped the English charts.

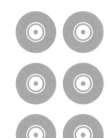

6

Gold certifications given to *OK Computer* in six different countries. It also has earned six platinum certifications.

3

The time (3 a.m.) when the song *Let Down* was recorded in a dance hall.

2007

The band's seventh album, *In Rainbows*, is launched online before being released as a record, through 'pay-what-you-want' downloads.

2018

Thom Yoke is chosen by Italian director Luca Guadagnino to create the soundtrack for his remake of Dario Argento's *Suspiria*.

Nirvana

Ecstasy in reverse, blinding illumination that is perhaps blind from the outset. Choosing a name like Nirvana in the late 1980s was like excluding all possibility of redemption. Jim Morrison had attempted to open the 'doors' of perception and probably burned his hand on the flames of hell on the other side of the threshold. It seemed that those doors could be opened easily, but it was clear that one would find only mediocre revelations, or rather, a devastating heap of adolescent dreams. Through their biting social commentary, Nirvana ridiculed clichés such as the idea that youth equates to being good-looking, bold and happy. Listening to the band, adolescents and adults alike were inspired to jump higher

216 KURT COBAIN, THE VOCALIST AND LEADER OF NIRVANA, ON STAGE IN READING WITH EUGENE KELLY OF THE VASELINES.

217 NIRVANA TAPING THEIR *MTV LIVE AND LOUD* TV SPECIAL IN DECEMBER 1993 AT PIER 28 IN SEATTLE. KURT COBAIN IS IN THE FOREGROUND. THE BAND EMERGED FROM THE SEATTLE GRUNGE SCENE TO ACHIEVE WORLDWIDE SUCCESS.

and higher until they cracked their head against the ceiling. Nirvana gave anyone who was willing to listen the urge to light fires and burn whatever was still alive in the wasteland of juvenile existence. It was an insane project, suburban satori, corrupt and irremediably gone astray. And it was no laughing matter. Today, an album like *Nevermind* is impossible to avoid; it's right there before your eyes, like an oxidized, well-worn monolith, bearing witness to a period that penetrated time like an impertinent wedge, something who-knows-where and who-knows-when that might return at any moment, especially when we least expect it, an act of celestial spite carried out by angels whose wings are soiled by petroleum.

And then there's rock, which in the America of the time was considered a putrid corpse, a metal pantomime used to hoodwink suckers, the fruit of a global market completely out of touch with younger generations, with the ideas and passion of those who still dreamed of combining poetry and rage through music. In the early 1990s, rock was apparently old hat, ready to be swept away by rap. But then came Nirvana, with their basic instruments (guitar, bass, percussion and voice), to embody just about everything: the invisible, the lost generation, those who had no identity and were no longer loved or listened to, those who rejected the status quo and would soon march along the streets of Seattle in protest.

Cobain did all this because he had to, because rock was in his blood, because his voice sprang from his throat almost in spite of itself, because he had no other choice. He didn't seek to represent a generation, he never spoke on anyone's behalf, and he did not want to be on stage as a star. He was a public figure, a life lived in public, his joy and pain was experienced, suffered and loved in public, and his music narrated everything he couldn't manage to say in words. And the public devoured and consumed him; it sucked his lifeblood and robbed him of his energy (just play *Smells Like a Teen Spirit* at full blast and see the effect it has on those listening). Twelve albums: three of them studio recordings (the ones that earned the band its success and legendary status), three live releases, and six collections. Eight years of activity up to Cobain's death, a wave of concerts, 75 million copies sold, and an unmistakable sound that sustained the frontman's lyrics and voice. Nirvana was a band that successfully merged punk, hard rock, heavy metal, indie, songwriting, melody, rebellion and utopia. And then came the tragedy of Cobain's suicide at the age of twenty-seven, crushed by the weight of a life he could no longer endure. What remains is his music, the band's songs, and the dream of rebellious, electrifying rock that will be loved for a long, long time to come.

NIRVANA

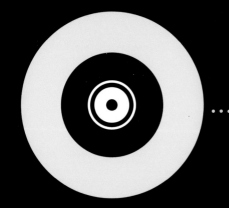

30

Album copies sold, in millions, of *Nevermind*, well beyond even the most optimistic expectations.

11,799

Amount, in dollars, a hotel had to pay out of its own pocket for property damage done by Kurt Loder and Krist Novoselic, who smashed the TV in a room and dragged its furniture into the lobby.

550

Amount, in dollars, that Kurt Cobain paid for a car bought from a friend who sold it cheap because he thought it looked like a car someone's grandma would drive. Cobain was forced to sleep in that automobile multiple times after he was evicted from his home.

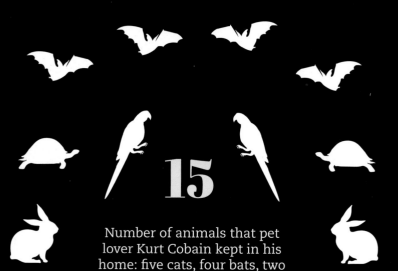

15

Number of animals that pet lover Kurt Cobain kept in his home: five cats, four bats, two parrots, two rabbits and two turtles.

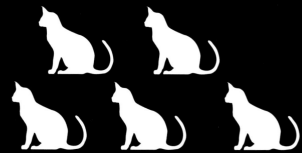

250,000

Number of copies of *Nevermind* estimated to be sold by the band's label.

27

Cobain's age when he committed suicide, adding his name to a long list of incredible musicians who died at this age (among the other members of the famous 'Club 27' were Brian Jones, Jimi Hendrix, Janis Joplin, Jim Morrison and, more recently, Amy Winehouse).

4

Age, in months, of the baby that Kirk Weddle photographed for the cover of *Nevermind*.

150

Amount earned, in dollars, by the parents of Spencer Eldon (the aforementioned baby) for having allowed their child to be photographed in a swimming pool.

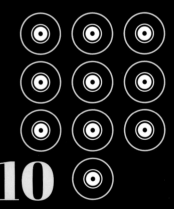

10

The total number of albums in the band's discography, three of which were studio recordings, three were live and four were compilations (three of which were posthumous).

6

Awards received by Nirvana from 1992 to 1995, including five MTV Video Music Awards and a Grammy (for Best Alternative Album).

Pearl Jam

Their songs are not mere songs. They are raging confessions, stances, love ballads, a handful of photographs taken god knows where, like are Polaroids that capture moments, images and thoughts, a marvelous catalog of the fascinating qualities of every single member of this band from Seattle. Yes, because Pearl Jam – Eddie Vedder, Jeff Ament, Mike McCready, Stone Gossard and Matt Cameron – are a real band, a unique collective that has functioned to perfection since 1990. Unlike most of their colleagues, these five musicians have a clear vision of what rock can be today, what power, messages and emotions it can transmit. And every time they return, with albums and concerts, they do so with the same spirit and passion as always, with music that looks toward the future without betraying the past. This holds true when they first formed the band (and even earlier, with Green River, Mother Love Bone and Temple of the Dog), because they have always attempted to combine, without going to far or forcing matters, the rock of yesterday and today into a single whole. As a result, punk and grunge, heavy metal and psychedelia, ballads and other types of songs, classic rock and pop exist in the music of Pearl Jam. But it's all combined into unique a sound that's brilliant and captivating, filled with surprising musical solutions, improvised openings and strong contrasts. To paraphrase the title of one of their albums, Pearl Jam's music is undeniably 'without a code'; it doesn't conform to a genre but rather pursues emotion. And although the band rightly earns the rock label again and again without confusion or compromise, it also eludes all the categories and genres that have been pre-established by the music industry. Following present-day trends, one might say

222-223   MATT CAMERON, EDDIE VEDDER AND STONE GOSSARD OF PEARL JAM PERFORMING AT FENWAY PARK IN BOSTON IN AUGUST 2016.

Pearl Jam

60

Total number of albums sold by *Pearl Jam* to date, in millions.

2001

A *Space Odyssey* (directed by Stanley Kubrick) is Eddie Vedder's favorite movie.

950,378

Copies sold of their second album, *Vs.* in the first week of its release, which took place on October 19, 1993.

261

Number of weeks that *Ten* remained on the top of the charts in the U.S., where the album sold more than ten million copies.

72

The number of 'official bootlegs' released from the band's 2,000 European and American tour dates. The copies of live bootleg albums sold up to 2008 totaled 3.5 million.

9

Number of victims of the tragedy that occurred on June 30 ,2000 at the Roskilde Festival in Denmark during Pearl Jam's performance. The crowd rushed toward the stage in pelting rain, crushing nine fans to death and injuring another 26.

6

Number of years Pearl Jam refused to make music videos – from the release of their first album to *Do the Evolution* (a single from the band's fifth album, *Yield*, released in 1998).

1

One year, the time it took *Ten* to reach 2nd place on the American charts.

1995

The year that Neil Young collaborated most with the band. Together they recorded *Mirror Ball*, one of Young's finest records from the 1990s.

1991

Pearl Jam's debut album *Ten* is released.

that Pearl Jam is an alternative rock band, removed from the commercial mainstream. But even this label doesn't do justice to their music, because, in one fell swoop, Pearl Jam overcame the insecurities and misunderstandings that arose once grunge was over, as well as the trends connected to it. Miraculously, the band was freed of the need to sum up or repeat what had already been said and done in the 1990s by a new, often rebellious generation of American rock musicians. Certainly, the band's evolution was also influenced by Vedder's experiences with the Pakistani Qawwali music vocalist Nusrat Fateh Ali Khan, when they worked together on *The Face of Love,* a song for the soundtrack of *Dead Man Walking* (directed by Tim Robbins), and his solo work for the soundtrack of another film, *Into the Wild.* Jeff Ament's collaboration with Three Fish, which produced music permeated with Sufism (the band's name was taken from

a poem by Rumi) also had an impact, as did the entire band's collaboration with Neil Young and with many other musicians who played with them over the years. Yet, generally speaking, what's counted most in the history of Pearl Jam was its rigor, coherence and consistency, and a love for rock, not as a genre but as an attitude and a way of dealing with life and music, together with its vast repertory of 'historic' references (from Led Zeppelin to the Doors, and from the Who to the Sex Pistols), which are the very framework of the band's oeuvre. In short, Pearl Jam's music isn't made for easy, rapid consumption or distracted listening. This isn't background music. Instead, they craft songs with depth and soul, songs in which the band seeks to combine poetry and passion, rage and melody, grief and hope, to reconstruct and no longer destroy, entertain while making the audience reflect – just as great rock has always done.

225 PEARL JAM, ANOTHER BAND THAT HELPED SHAPE THE GRUNGE SCENE FROM THE LATE 1980S TO THE EARLY 1990S, DURING A CONCERT AT BONNAROO IN MANCHESTER, TENNESSEE (2008).

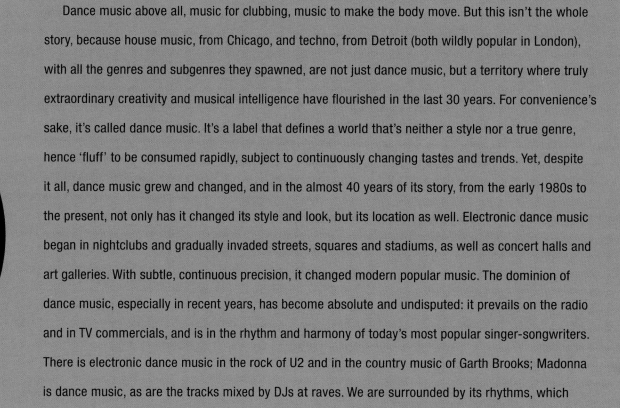

Techno & House

Dance music above all, music for clubbing, music to make the body move. But this isn't the whole story, because house music, from Chicago, and techno, from Detroit (both wildly popular in London), with all the genres and subgenres they spawned, are not just dance music, but a territory where truly extraordinary creativity and musical intelligence have flourished in the last 30 years. For convenience's sake, it's called dance music. It's a label that defines a world that's neither a style nor a true genre, hence 'fluff' to be consumed rapidly, subject to continuously changing tastes and trends. Yet, despite it all, dance music grew and changed, and in the almost 40 years of its story, from the early 1980s to the present, not only has it changed its style and look, but its location as well. Electronic dance music began in nightclubs and gradually invaded streets, squares and stadiums, as well as concert halls and art galleries. With subtle, continuous precision, it changed modern popular music. The dominion of dance music, especially in recent years, has become absolute and undisputed: it prevails on the radio and in TV commercials, and is in the rhythm and harmony of today's most popular singer-songwriters. There is electronic dance music in the rock of U2 and in the country music of Garth Brooks; Madonna is dance music, as are the tracks mixed by DJs at raves. We are surrounded by its rhythms, which

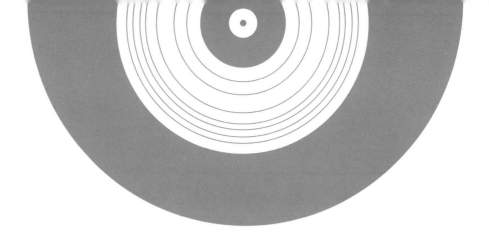

also permeate cell phone ring tones and popular movie soundtracks. The ubiquity of electronic dance music certainly is not restricted to the Western world; it is also part and parcel of the music scene in Africa, Asia, and the Middle East – a revolution, an unstoppable avalanche, a relentless wave that has overwhelmed everyone and everything, forcing even the noblest minds of modern music to reckon with its digital reality. Dance music, especially the electronic variety, is the rock of the new millennium, the music of teenagers whose parents consider it nothing more than 'noise'. It's a sound and rhythm that grew out of youth culture that broke with the past, turning DJs into the new heroes of popular music, musicians who don't play traditional instruments, yet produce gold records and fill stadiums. Electronic dance music, which was born just after the rise of disco music, has a long history and many different 'souls'. There's house, the music of its origins, conceived in Chicago and then developed in the hands of London disc jockeys. There's techno, which was created in the clubs of Detroit, changing the musical customs of two generations. There's the most popular dance music of all, the one that topped and tops the charts and sells millions of records. And lastly, there are the many genres and subgenres that are beloved by a large, passionate and attentive audience around the globe. Dance music has generated a large number of stars, hundreds of successful songs and a true youth culture, becoming the soundtrack of the present day.

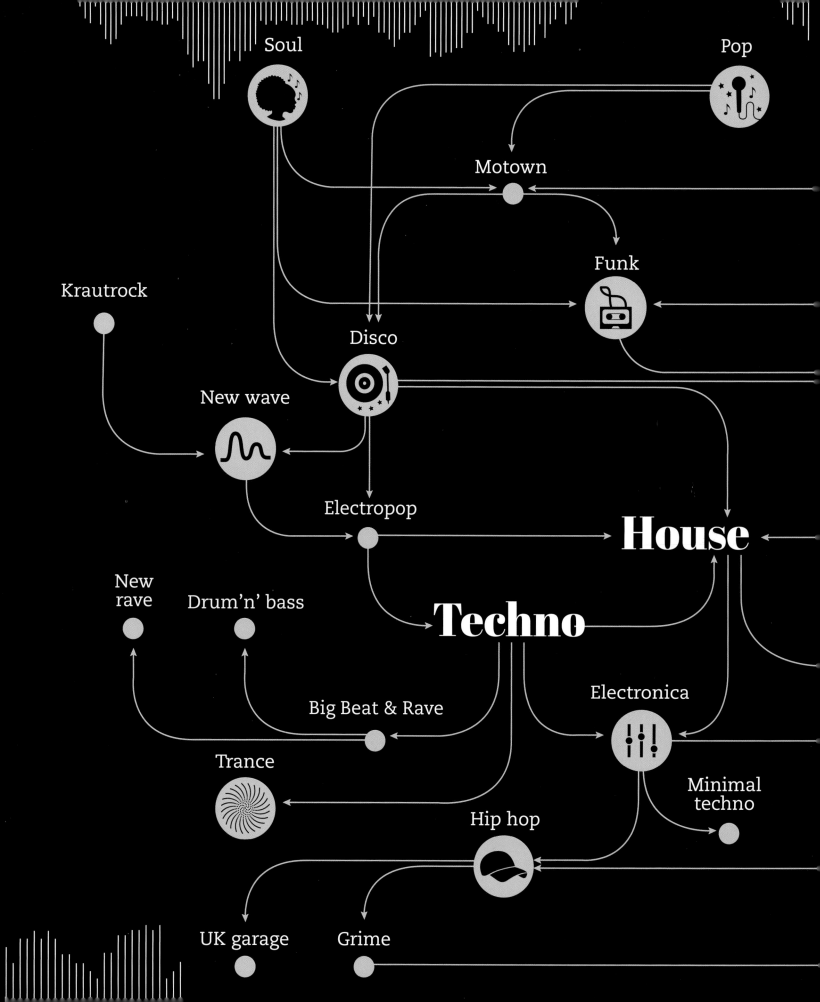

Rhythm 'n' blues

Calypso

Rock

Reggae

Old school
hip hop

Techno
& House

Trip hop

Dubstep

The chemical brothers

125,000

Number of spectators at the Oasis concert in Knebworth, where the Chemical Brothers were the opening act.

21

Times, in millions, that *Galvanize* has been played on Spotify.

9

Number of studio albums released by the band.

2

Chemical Brothers singles that have topped the English charts.

1989

The year Rowlands and Simons began working together.

1995

The year the band changed its name to the Chemical Brothers.

1997

The band wins a Grammy with *Block Rockin' Beats*.

1  live

The Chemical Brothers have only one live album: *Don't Think*.

2005

The Chemical Brothers win another Grammy with *Galvanize*.

1999

The year *Hey Boy, Hey Girl* is released.

The Chemical Brothers

Once upon a time there was rock. It was plugged in, played with a guitar and shouted by gritty singers. It was adored by teens and adolescents, who identified with it. Then came electronic keyboards, and yesterday's rock suddenly got old. This marked the beginning of house, techno, digital, and computer music, and sound became increasingly hi-tech. Then came the DJs, and guitars were put out to pasture. In the 1990s, rock and technology found a meeting point with the arrival of a new generation of bands who interpreted the passion of rock with a new sound: the Prodigy, Faithless, Underworld and, above all, the Chemical Brothers. Many years have passed since the duo's debut but Tom Rowlands and Ed Simons have not abandoned their characteristic style; they are still DJs first and musicians second. They stated that the idea of becoming DJs came to them when they were still quite young. It encapsulated everything they wanted to do: work in a club, make people dance, ensuring the audience was entertained and partied til they dropped. And they're still happy to do just that. Raves may be passé, but the spirit with which the Chemical Brothers continue to make music is exactly the same, a combination of good feelings, great rhythm, intense pulsation, avant-garde technology, and amazing sounds based on a beat that stirs both the body and soul. The reference point is techno, but for those who think that techno is only niche dance music, the Chemical Brothers demonstrate that one can aim much higher, describing and defining our age and the sentiments of a generation. Through their albums and concerts, Rowlands and Simons have tried to present the true nature of a hidden, mysterious generation: Generation X. They have guided us through rites and myths, the language of the body and of machines, through a world that was being built before our very eyes to the technological rhythm of highly original music.

And to this day, although the Chemical Brothers' music has lost some of its original luster, they are still fascinating and captivating DJ/musicians who envision the soundtrack of our times. As they say, there is no difference between being DJs and musicians. The music they create is theirs; they still like playing it and making people happy as they listen to it, both in the studio and on stage. In fact, they say that concerts are the best way for people to really hear and understand what they have to offer.

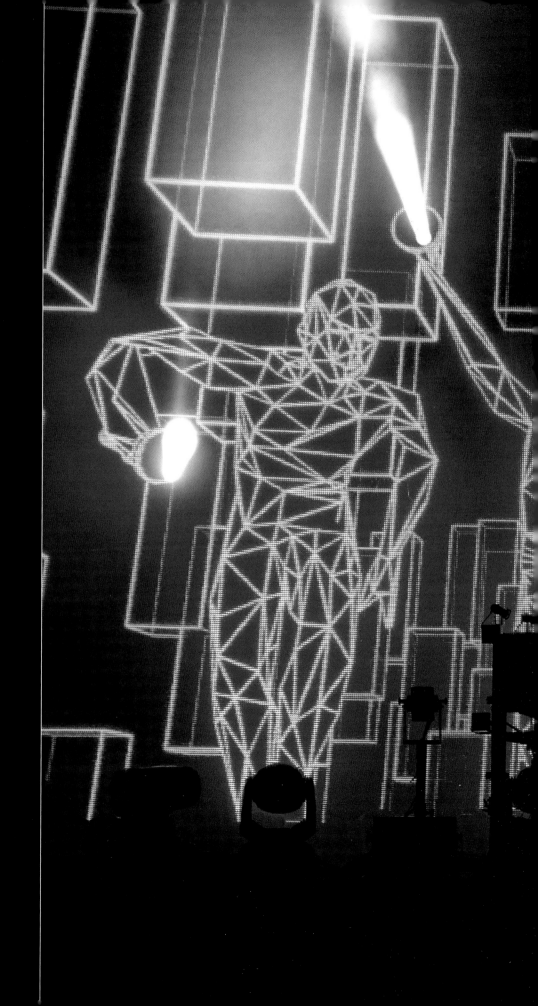

222-223 ED SIMONS (LEFT) AND TOM ROWLANDS (RIGHT) PERFORMING WITH THE CHEMICAL BROTHERS ON THE MUNDO STAGE ON THE THIRD DAY OF THE ROCK IN RIO FESTIVAL IN LISBON, PORTUGAL IN 2018.

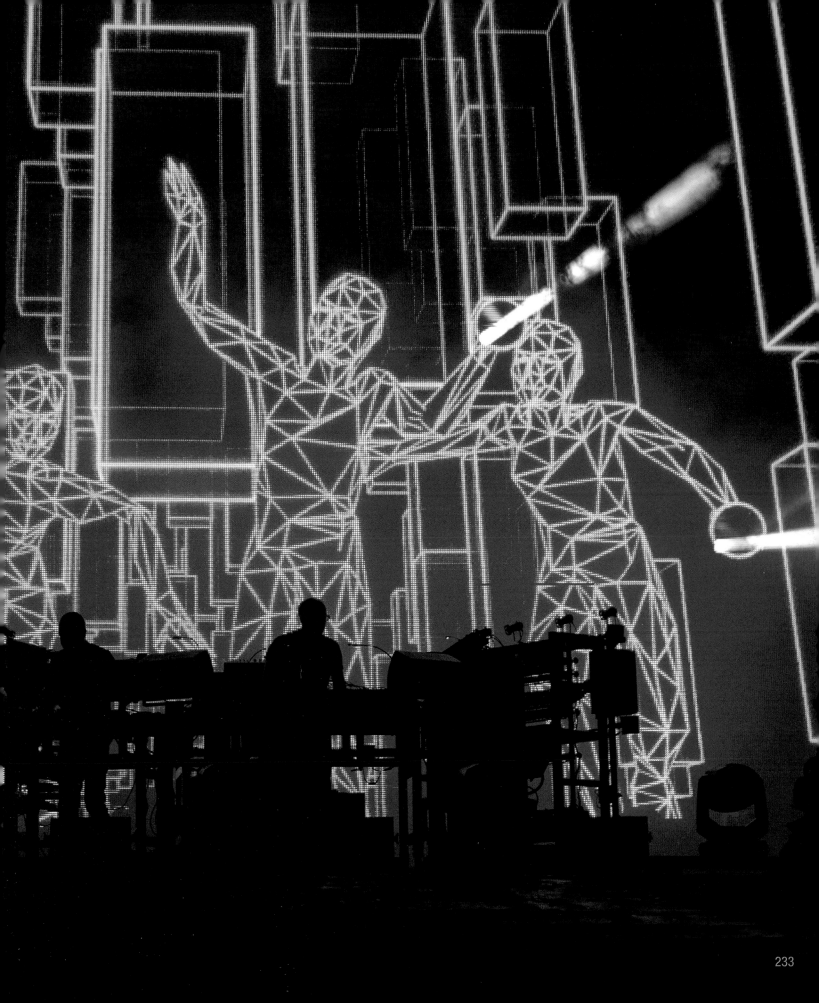

Daft Punk

It's called EDM, an acronym for electronic dance music, which can be heard every night in nightclubs and bars, on beaches, and in squares and stadiums. It's the music that tops the charts and makes everyone dance to the beat, especially in summer. Its stars are a new generation of DJs and electronic musicians, from Deadmau5 to Avicii, from Tiesto to Apparat. Such artists interpret EDM in their own personal fashion, touching upon pop and avant-garde, going from obsessive, pulsating rhythms to ethereal, intangible atmospheres. This is the sound of the dawn of the third millennium, an electronic beat that has deeply changed how we create, perform, experience and listen to music. This is 'machine-made' music that not only reproduces the sounds of instruments but also creates new ones, constantly, in a combination of infinite bits and bytes. Forty years ago, Kraftwerk emerged from Düsseldorf to establish the rules of this genre, which have not really changed to any significant extent since then. Kraftwerk's music was visionary and influenced an entire generation of musicians thanks to experimentation. Now, after passing through myriad variations, that vision is here again with Daft Punk. The members of this French duo, Guy-Manuel de Homen-Christo and Thomas Bangalter, have been friends since high school and have performed together since 1992. With them, techno, house and dance music have gone mainstream;

their creative and sophisticated approach has merged dance music and art. Daft Punk has transformed the 'computer world' of Kraftwerk into music that is imaginative, danceable, and electronic, yet animated by sentiment and passion, anything but cold and mechanical. On the contrary, it may even feel 'analog', as if the robots impersonated by the bandmates (whose faces are covered with futuristic helmets, making them unrecognizable and almost non-human) wanted to place life at the center of pop. The circle is completed: "We were trying to make robotic voices sound the most human they've ever sounded, in terms of expressivity and emotion," said Bangalter.

Music has become the offspring of machines in every recording studio or small room where any kid with a computer can mix elements by using cut and paste, sequencers, synthesizers, samplers and drum machines. In the 1990s, the media talked only about rap and hip hop, yet DJs attracted millions to Berlin's *Love Parade,* and they did so via the techno and house music that was already being played in the 1980s. Daft Punk returned to Giorgio Moroder, to Nile Rodgers of Chic, to the sounds of Michael Jackson's *Thriller* (another electronic masterpiece of the 1980s) to reinvent the future of dance music. And to make sure that the man-machine dreamed of by Kraftwerk came to life, not thanks to an electronic circuitboard, but to a heartbeat.

234   DAFT PUNK, WITH THEIR TRADEMARK FUTURISTIC HELMETS COVERING THEIR FACES, WHILE PERFORMING AT COACHELLA IN INDIO, CALIFORNIA IN APRIL 2006.

Daft Punk

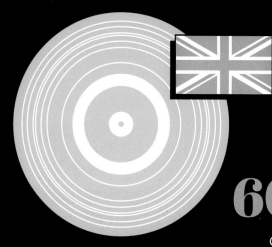

7

Copies of *Get Lucky* sold worldwide, in millions.

600,000

Copies of *One More Time* sold in England.

▶ **56**

Views, in millions, of the fan-generated video version of *Harder, Better, Faster, Stronger.*

1992

The year Darlin', the first band of the Daft Punk duo, is formed.

1996

The year the duo decide to conceal their faces for good.

2000

The year *One More Time,* is released, their first single to enter the Top 40 in the U.S.

2001

Discovery is released.

74 The minutes of playing time of *Random Access Memory*, the maximum duration of a CD.

65,000
The amount, in dollars, spent to make the helmets used in the video for *Discovery*.

10'32" Runtime of the remix of *Get Lucky*.

 12

Guy-Manuel de Homem-Christo and Thomas Bangalter's age when they met.

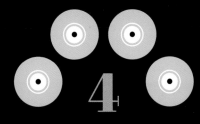 **4**

Studio albums the band has released.

2010
The year Daft Punk produces the soundtrack for *Tron: Legacy*.

2005

The band wins a Grammy Award with *Human after All*.

2014

The single *Get Lucky* wins two Grammy Awards, and the album *Random Access Memory* another two.

The Authors

Ernesto Assante became a journalist in 1977. During a career spanning over 30 years, he has contributed to many Italian and foreign weeklies and monthlies including *Epoca*, *L'Espresso*, and *Rolling Stone*. He created and oversaw the supplements Musica, Computer Valley, and Computer, Internet e Altro for the Italian daily *La Repubblica*. Assante has also written books on music criticism, often in collaboration with his colleague Gino Castaldo. Since 2005, Assante and Castaldo have hosted Lessons in Rock: Journey to the Center of Music, a series of multimedia presentations that delve into the history and legendary figures of rock music. From 2003 to 2009, Assante taught at Sapienza University in Rome. His classes included Theory and Technique of New Media and Analysis of Musical Languages. He has written numerous important books for White Star Publishers.

Giulia De Amicis. After completing a master's degree in communication design in 2012, Giulia began working as a visual designer and illustrator. Her work primarily consists of presenting information visually for newspapers, magazines, and associations in the environmental sector, with a particular focus on marine ecology, geography, and human rights. She has recently illustrated several publications for White Star Kids.

Photo Credits

Project editor
Valeria Manferto De Fabianis

Editorial Assistant
Giorgia Raineri

Graphic design
Maria Cucchi

WHITE STAR PUBLISHERS

WS White Star Publishers® is a registered trademark property of White Star s.r.l.

© 2019 White Star s.r.l.
Piazzale Luigi Cadorna, 6 - 20123 Milan, Italy
www.whitestar.it

Translation: Richard Pierce - Editing: Katherine Kirby

ISBN 978-88-544-1533-1
2 3 4 5 6   24 23 22 21 20

Printed in Slovenia